COUNSELING HELPSHEETS

by

Tom Klaus

and

Lamar Roth

Group®

Loveland, Colorado

Counseling Helpsheets
Copyright © 1994 Tom Klaus and Lamar Roth

Credits
Edited by Lois Keffer
Cover designed by Liz Howe
Cover photography by Steven W. Jones, FPG International
Designed by Jean Bruns

Scriptures quoted from The Everyday Bible, New Century Version, copyright © 1987, 1988 by Word Publishing, Dallas, Texas 75039. Used by permission.

Library of Congress Cataloging-in-Publication Data
Klaus, Tom, 1954–
    Counseling helpsheets / by Tom Klaus and Lamar Roth.
      p.   cm.
    ISBN 1-55945-007-X
    1. Teenagers—Pastoral counseling of. 2. Church work with
teenagers. I. Roth, Lamar, 1958– . II. Title.
    BV4447.K58 1994
    259'.23—dc20
                             94-36
                             CIP

11 10 9 8 7 6 5 4 3 2   04 03 02 01 00 99 98 97 96 95

ISBN 1-55945-007-X
Printed in the United States of America.

Contents

Introduction

"*Can you help me?*"

Mandy's eyes teared as her quivering lips whispered the plea. Julia, a youth worker, felt totally inadequate as she stared mutely at the struggling teenager before her. When Julia made no response, Mandy's broken voice repeated the question, *"Please . . . can you help me?"*

This is one of the toughest questions ever asked of youth workers. And it evokes within us a variety of responses. We want to help. We want to give comfort and wise counsel and point kids toward God's best solutions. But there are many times when we just don't know where to begin.

Those who experience a feeling of inadequacy may respond in a way that intensifies the teenager's sense of hopelessness. Fear, and its ensuing panic, may result in a response that appears to be nothing more than cruel silence.

The other, equally dangerous extreme is offering more assistance than we're able to deliver. This is especially tempting to those who perceive themselves as possessing unique powers in ministry. Before long, they're likely to find themselves floundering right along with the teenager they're trying to help.

The good news is that the skills pastors and youth workers need to respond appropriately to teenagers' pleas for help are well within reach. A sense of humility and a genuine love for kids, combined with a basic understanding of counseling principles, can empower you to offer help and hope.

And, simply stated, that's the purpose of this book—to equip youth workers and pastors to offer answers of hope to the teenagers under their care. As a pastor or youth worker, it's likely that you already possess two of the three essential qualities of an effective counselor—a genuine love for kids and the humility of one called by God to ministry.

In this book we offer you the third essential—a basic understanding of counseling principles that will help you step into counseling situations with confidence. Here are a few things we'd like to share with you as you begin.

First, we've been where you are. Together we have nearly 30 years of experience as professional youth ministers. Like Julia, we have been frozen by the *"Can you help me?"* question. Sometimes we were saved by fast thinking and replies that seemed to help for the moment. Occasionally, by the grace of God, responses tumbled from our mouths before we had a chance to think, yet the words we heard ourselves speak offered life and hope. But most often we were stuck without a clue about what to do next.

Those experiences have pushed us into different ministries. Today, Lamar is a clinical psychologist who specializes in the treatment of children and adolescents. Tom is a private-practice mental-health counselor and prevention educator whose work brings him into daily contact with adolescents. Both of us are active in local churches and hold ordination from our respective denominations. We share a deep respect for the role of youth ministry in healing brokenness and transforming lives.

Second, we acknowledge that you are the expert in youth ministry. While we've worked in youth ministry in the past, today we are trained professional therapists/counselors. We believe this is an important distinction to be maintained in this book. Our past experience only qualifies us to offer insights into youth ministry. You will decide what, of all we offer, is relevant to your situation.

Likewise, we believe it's important for you to maintain a distinction between your role and ours. Unless you're trained and qualified as a therapist, it's important not to represent yourself as a professional counselor, nor to assume that role with members of your congregation.

Why is this is so important? Simple ethics tell us it's wrong for people to represent themselves as something they're not. And from a legal standpoint, there are grave implications for false representation of credentials and skills. We'll discuss these two crucial issues later in this section.

Third, we offer this book as a helpful tool with a caution that it won't transform a pastor or youth worker into a professional counselor. In fact, we have consciously steered clear of using a professional counseling model as we describe the church worker's role in a helping relationship. Instead, we've provided another model for you to use in personal helping relationships with your teenagers.

AN OVERVIEW

Counseling Helpsheets is laid out in three sections.

The first section (you are here!) lays a foundation for what follows. We begin by introducing you to the model of helping we mentioned above. Then we deal in more depth with key ethical and legal issues in helping relationships. Becoming well-acquainted with this information will help you use and apply the rest of the book most effectively.

The middle section of the book is a hands-on reference you'll find to be invaluable when teenagers come to you with problems. We've identified dozens of personal and family problems a youth worker is likely to confront. Each problem is addressed on a two-page spread. On the first page of each spread you'll find several tips on how to approach the problem, what you're likely to hear, how best to respond, and how to follow up.

The facing page of each spread is a photocopiable work sheet to use with kids who are seeking your help. The work sheets provide an agenda for talking with kids, so you won't have to worry about feeling lost or inadequate. The questions on each work sheet help teenagers clarify the problem, identify and express feelings about the problem, and develop a strategy for dealing with it. The last section of each work sheet includes Scriptures and follow-up ideas for kids to read and use after you've met together.

The final section of the book helps you recognize problems that require referral to a mental-health professional such as a physician, psychiatrist, psychologist, psychotherapist, clinical social worker, counselor, or family therapist. We'll name specific behaviors that help you know when kids have entered a danger zone and need professional help. We'll also explain how to find competent professionals and how to make a good referral.

Some issues appear in both the second and third sections of the book. That's because many common problems occur in varying degrees of severity. We believe there are some potentially serious problems you can handle with great success, especially if they're identified and addressed in the earliest stages. In fact, some serious crises can be averted altogether through early detection and intervention.

When a particular problem appears in both sections of the book, we'll be very specific about the extent of your helping role. In the middle section we'll explain exactly how to tackle the problem, then alert you when it's wisest to step back and make a referral. We'll also explain how to assume a supportive role while a mental-health professional takes over primary care.

HERE'S TO YOU!

As a church worker, you may be the first person a teenager comes to in times of personal or family difficulty. This places you in a privileged role that offers you access to the lives and hearts of kids in a way that's unparalleled by almost any other profession. Our goal with this book is to help you rise to your highest potential in one of the most crucial ministries you'll ever perform—the ministry of caring.

Part One:
THE MINISTRY OF CARING

A Way of Helping:
THE MINISTRY OF CARING

The "ministry of caring" is how we'll refer to our model for working with young people who come to you for help. We believe this approach is well-suited to the unique relationships and responsibilities of people in ministerial roles. You'll find this model to be somewhat different from techniques used in professional counseling.

We realize that our position may differ from what writers of other counseling books have to say. While we honor and respect their opinions, we are convinced that this approach is most appropriate for those in ministry roles.

We offer this practical, legal, and ethical basis for our approach.

■ From a practical standpoint, our experience in church work has taught us that most ministers and youth workers simply don't have time to fill the role of counselor. While some may have time to provide *occasional* counsel, their already over-burdened schedules don't allow them to commit to hours of counseling week after week. The challenge of ministering to the congregation or the youth group as a whole can quickly become overbalanced by a demanding relationship with one or two individuals.

■ Legally, the recent explosion of lawsuits makes counseling a risky business for even the most highly trained and qualified professional. In light of a clear trend to make ministers more accountable to the law when they take on counseling roles, we propose that you discourage people from seeing you as a professional counselor or therapist. It takes wisdom and forethought to prevent your earnest desire to help from placing you in a legally compromising situation.

■ The ethical perspective is fairly straightforward. It is not in anyone's best interest when people present themselves as professionals in fields in which they lack specific training and credentials. Getting entangled in a difficult counseling situation can, in fact, be potentially damaging to people, your reputation, and the reputation of your church.

Are we saying that a counseling ministry should be struck completely from your agenda? Not at all! We propose the ministry of caring as an appropriate and effective means of helping teenagers who come to you and ask, *"Can you help me?"*

The concept of the ministry of caring is inspired by the biblical example of Joseph of Cyprus, an early convert to Christianity who lived for a time in Jerusalem. He is first mentioned in Acts 4:36, just prior to the better-known story of Ananias and Sapphira.

Joseph sold a field and donated the proceeds to the apostles for the support of the Christian community. His act of generosity probably inspired Ananias and Sapphira, who likewise sold a field but held back part of the proceeds and were struck dead for their deceit. This dramatic incident in the life of the early church introduces us to Joseph of Cyprus. Other Scriptures tell us that Joseph played an essential role in caring for members of the Christian community.

Does he sound familiar? Probably not, unless you're aware of the new name given Joseph by the apostles. In the tradition of biblical name changes, Joseph's new name described his essential character: Barnabas, the son of consolation or son of encouragement. A brief look at the life of Barnabas shows how his ministry, as well as his name, are the inspiration for the ministry of caring.

Barnabas is mentioned by name in the book of Acts 29 times. His place in church history is distinguished by the way he cared for people. Barnabas was a comforting, caring presence in the lives of the apostles; Paul; John Mark; the believers in Cyprus, Pamphylia, and Galatia; and the church in Antioch. Barnabas had a unique ministry of "being there" for people who needed him. It is his ministry of presence, or being there, that serves as our model for the ministry of caring.

With the example of Barnabas in mind, let's look at three specific ways the ministry of caring helps us give answers of hope to people in need.

The Ministry of Caring 1:
LISTENING

The ministry of caring begins, to state it simply, when we shut our mouths and open our ears. Listening is the first of three important skills in the art of being there for people.

Listening is important because it helps us gain some understanding of the person's story, his or her feelings at the moment, and the needs that must be addressed.

For most people, listening skills don't come easily or naturally. So how do we listen to a teenager who comes to us for help?

■ **First, and most obviously, we listen with our ears.** We let the person tell his or her story, and we take in every word of it. Our goal in listening with our ears is to understand as accurately as possible the issue that prompted the person to seek our help.

Paraphrasing is an effective technique that helps you hear with understanding. When you paraphrase, you simply rephrase the gist of what you heard. That is, you express the person's thought or story in your own words and see how the person responds. If the response is, "Yeah, that's it," you know you've been hearing accurately. If the response is, "No, I meant . . ." you have an opportunity to listen again and repeat the process until you understand clearly what the person is saying.

Here's an example of how paraphrasing works.

TRACY: I . . . well . . . saw Steve last Friday night after the ballgame and got home kind of late.

YOU: You had a date with Steve and missed your curfew.

TRACY: Well, uh, I, uh, really missed my curfew. I didn't get home until about 7 in the morning.

YOU: You spent the night with Steve on Friday. You seem really upset about that.

TRACY: Yes. We had sex.

As you can see, paraphrasing not only helps you understand the story as clearly as possible, it will sometimes help people find the words they need to say difficult things.

It's important to paraphrase only when you aren't clear about what the person is saying. If, in the case above, Tracy had said, "Steve and I had sex last Friday night," a paraphrase of her statement wouldn't have been necessary. In fact, if you paraphrase when the meaning is already clear, you will appear to be playing some kind of cruel game of words. And the person who sought your help will begin to feel frustrated by your repeated interruptions.

You listen with your ears for content, for what is being said. You also listen for silence, for what's being left out—the untold story.

For example, a student may drop by to talk to you about a problem at home. You notice he talks about every family member except his mom. His silence about his mother should prompt you to ask yourself, "Why is he leaving her out? Is the mother living at home? Is there an ongoing tension or feud between the boy and his mother? Is there something about his mother that he's too angry or ashamed or embarrassed to risk revealing?"

Any time you listen to a person's story and you hear silence where there should logically be content, you need to check it out.

In the instance above, you could do this by asking, "Have you talked to your mom about this?" His response will tell you a lot. In other situations, you may need to be more or less direct in checking out the untold story.

Listening with our ears helps us understand the person's story. It may also help us understand how someone is feeling at the moment. But we often get a better understanding of people's feelings as we listen with our eyes.

■ **When we listen with our eyes we begin to know how people's stories are affecting them.** Consider again the exchange with Tracy. By her halting speech and the way she approached the subject indirectly, you know she was feeling awkward and somewhat embarrassed. Now, with the visual clues added, see how her deeper feelings are revealed.

TRACY: *(Eyes avoiding yours, face flushed)* I . . . well . . . saw Steve last Friday night after the ballgame and got home kind of late.

YOU: You had a date with Steve and missed your curfew.

TRACY: *(Looking down, wringing her hands)* Well, uh, I, uh, really missed my curfew. I didn't get home until about 7 in the morning.

YOU: You spent the night with Steve on Friday. You seem really upset about that.

TRACY: *(A tear drops onto her hand.)* Yes. We had sex.

What do your eyes tell you about Tracy's feelings? The flush and hand wringing tell you she feels awkward and embarrassed. But the averted eyes and tears tell you she may be feeling the deeper emotions of shame and grief.

People's bodies tell us a lot about their feelings. Clenched jaws and fists reveal anger. Wide eyes show excitement or fear. Fidgeting shows nervousness and discomfort. Hunched shoulders can indicate weariness or shame. A slumped posture can suggest a lack of interest and boredom. The list of body signals can go on and on, which brings us to an important point.

How a person communicates his or her story is just as important as the story itself.

So watch people as they talk with you. Our bodies tend to punctuate our words and give important clues about the intensity of our feelings.

Sometimes the absence of appropriate body language can also give a clue about the intensity of feelings. So watch for times when body language doesn't match the intensity of the story.

For example, Jeremy showed absolutely no emotion as he described to his youth group leader the horrible death of his puppy. The pup, which Jeremy had picked out at an animal shelter only a month before, had chewed up his dad's expensive new running shoes. In his anger, Jeremy's dad carried the dog to the back yard and shot it in the head with a small rifle, even as Jeremy begged his father to let the dog go.

In this situation, Jeremy's flat expression spoke volumes about the depth of his feelings. This ability to discuss horrifying personal happenings without apparent emotion is common when a person has experienced emotional trauma or shock.

Our ears help us understand the story, and our eyes help us understand feelings. But to understand a person's need at the moment, we must listen with our heart.

■ **Listening with the heart involves what some people call "a sixth sense."** But there's more to it than just intuition.

To listen with the heart is to pay attention to ourselves and to the Spirit of God within us.

> *We pay attention to ourselves by being aware of our reactions to all that we are hearing through our ears and eyes. We pay attention to God's Spirit as we silently invite the presence and wisdom of God to the meeting.*

You've probably done this many times. We experience listening with our hearts as a process of internal questioning and answering. The key questions seem to be these:

1. What am I feeling as I listen to this person?

It is a myth that counselors have to shut off their own feelings to be effective. Counselors are human, too. We experience our own feelings as we hear another's story. Learn to be aware of your own feelings. They can guide you to better understand how you can help.

2. Am I feeling this because it's what the speaker is feeling, or do my feelings originate from my own problems?

The ability to feel what people experience as they tell their stories is known as empathic listening. But what we're feeling may have little or nothing to do with the feelings of the person telling the story. Our feelings may simply be shadows and ghosts of unresolved personal issues that the speaker's story conjures up in our minds.

The ability to discern the difference is a skill with which few people are gifted but most can learn. It takes practice, practice, and more practice.

Identifying the origin of your feelings as you counsel someone isn't easy. But here's a rule of thumb we've found helpful:

> *If our feelings are making it difficult to give focused attention to the speaker, then they originate in our own problems. If what we are feeling does not interfere with but perhaps even enhances our ability to focus, it is usually empathic listening.*

While this may be oversimplifying a complicated process, it should at least put us on the right track. Knowing the origin of our feelings is important because empathic listening helps us answer the next question.

3. If I'm feeling what the speaker is feeling, what do I need right now to feel consoled?

No, you didn't misread the question. It does not ask you to consider what the other needs. You see, this question recognizes that you've been listening empathically. For if you are feeling what the speaker is feeling, it's reasonable to assume that what consoles you will console him or her.

This assumption helps you know how to respond immediately to the speaker. For example, if you're feeling sad as you listen to the person, you may want to respond by saying, "I wonder if you're feeling sad" or "It seems so sad." When your response is on the mark, you will usually know by the speaker's acknowledgment or easy continuation of the story.

But what if you're wrong? Perhaps the person isn't feeling sad at all. Because the person wants to be heard by you, he or she will correct you. "No, I'm not really feeling sad, but I am feeling hurt." Don't interpret corrections as failure on your part. As you let every exchange teach you about the person, you will be better able to listen empathically to his or her story.

Listening with our ears, eyes, and heart is a critical skill in the ministry of consolation. Any time we're not sure we're hearing accurately, we need to check it out with the speaker. People's lives are too important for us to assume too much. The listening process described here may take only a few minutes, or it may take an hour.

The length of time spent listening is never as important as the feeling of being heard.

When people feel heard, they're better

prepared to take the next step in the ministry of consolation.

The Ministry of Caring 2:
DECISION MAKING

People often seek counseling because they don't know what to do in the face of a problem or difficult situation. So when they feel you've heard and understood their story, they'll want to know what comes next. *"Well, what do you think I should do?"* and *"Where do I go from here?"* are questions you're likely to hear.

In most cases people would like you to fix the problem for them, either by telling them what to do or by acting on their behalf. You cannot afford to do either. As a minister of caring, your role is to be there as a supportive presence while people work through their own problems.

It is in the process of resolving their own problems that people ultimately find healing and growth.

People who seek counseling often feel out of control in their lives, lacking any direction or ability to choose. In most cases your role will be to help them discover a direction and find the confidence to take the first steps. As they do this, you will see them attain a greater sense of confidence and self-esteem and a greater willingness to take responsibility for themselves.

While you can't make decisions or take action for people, you can help them through a decision-making process. This process should help people answer three questions for themselves.

1. *What do I need right now?*

2. *How does this fit with what I understand to be God's will for me at this time?*

3. *What will I do to get what I need?*

You'll be most effective guiding people through this process when you hold firmly to a deep faith in the grace of God. This means trusting that God is at work even when the decisions people make are not the ones you would choose.

There will be times, perhaps many, when you may re-create the scene from Luke 18:18-25 with someone who comes to you for help. In this story, a man asked Jesus, "What must I do to have life forever?" After hearing that the man had kept all the commandments since he was young, Jesus replied, "There is still one more thing you need to do. Sell everything you have and give it to the poor, and you will have treasure in heaven. Then come and follow me." Saddened, the man went away, for he was quite wealthy.

This story reminds us that not every counseling situation will have a happy ending. People who come to you may or may not be satisfied with your responses. Likewise, you may not agree with people's decisions. Sometimes decisions may involve a tough choice between two or more really bad options. Or, the person's plan may not work because it requires the cooperation of an unwilling third party.

In light of these possibilities, it's important to trust God's grace and allow events to unfold as they must. Your deep faith that God is at work frees you to empower people to take responsibility for their own problems through personal decision making. You are not the person who is finally responsible.

Once a decision has been made, your faith in God's grace doesn't mean you should sit back and do nothing. Some of your most vital work is done in the third, and final, component of the ministry of caring.

AUTHORS' NOTE: You'll find an excellent guide for the decision-making process in Friend to Friend, *a book by veteran youth workers J. David Stone and Larry Keefauver, published by YMTN-Stone & Associates. This book provides a simple yet effective method any youth worker or minister can use to help people make decisions. We encourage you to consider purchasing this excellent resource.*

The Ministry of Caring 3:
SUPPORTING

Providing support is anything but an inactive process. There are two important rules for providing support to people who are working through problems. The first is: Never do for people what they are capable of doing for themselves. The second is: Give the type of support that allows the person to retain the greatest power of choice.

Let's consider how these rules determine the level of support we offer as ministers of caring.

RULE #1: Never do for people what they are capable of doing for themselves.

This rule is rooted in the philosophy that people heal and grow as they take responsibility for their decisions, choices, and actions. It may be easier to be the doer rather than the encourager. And you may become impatient as people learn by trial and error what you already know. But the growth they'll experience in the process will be invaluable.

So you wait patiently while the person you're helping makes umpteen attempts to resolve a problem. But once the resolution is accomplished, won't that person feel more competent for what he or she has done? You know the answer because you've learned by experience, too. When someone fixes a problem for you, you feel relieved that the problem is gone. But you may also feel disempowered, as though you aren't able to take care of yourself. As a result, you're less inclined to take responsibility for yourself in the future.

One issue that counterbalances the rule of personal empowerment is the fact that teenagers may be limited in their ability to act on their own behalf by their position as legal minors. For example, it may be reasonable to expect a student to talk to a teacher by himself about what he perceives as an unfair grade. But it may be too much to expect a student to talk to her parents alone about a pregnancy.

Here are some other factors that may determine how involved you become in resolving a teenager's problem:

■ *the capabilities of the person, including age and physical or mental disabilities;*

■ *the nature of the problem and the degree to which the problem is impairing the person's ability to function; and*

■ *the risk of violence in the person's situation.*

A strong commitment to letting people do as much as they can for themselves will help you know how to follow the second rule.

RULE #2: Give the type of support that allows the person to retain the greatest power of choice.

We believe the ministry of caring allows you to offer five different types of support without crossing the line between minister and professional counselor. We'll go over these five types of support, then refer to them frequently in the second section of the book. In that section we'll explain which types of support are most appropriate for particular counseling issues.

Think of these five types of support on a continuum from the least power of choice to the most power of choice for the person seeking help. In other words, the type of support you provide will determine the amount of choice the person retains in dealing with his or her problem. Remember, our focus is not your level of power as a helper, but on retaining the person's maximum power of choice. (See the chart below.)

REFERRAL

Sometimes the best support you can give is to send a teenager to someone else for help. When you do this you are making a referral. Because you are acting for the person, referral provides the least power of choice. You may not always negotiate a referral or receive a person's permission. The decision to refer is often yours alone, based on your best judgment of the need at the moment.

There are many good reasons to send people elsewhere for help. You may suspect their problems require a level of professional assistance you're not qualified to provide. Or, they may need services your church doesn't offer. You may feel uncomfortable dealing with the particular issue they're trying to resolve. It may be difficult for you to work with some people because you don't like them. Sometimes you may feel a counseling relationship with a person

in your church is awkward because of the office or position that person holds.

Whatever your reason for making a referral, it's important that you see it as an option in any counseling situation at any time. The best time to refer is any time you feel the person would be better served through a referral.

In Part Three we'll examine a number of issues that almost always require immediate referral. We'll also provide helpful tips on making a good referral.

ADVOCACY

An advocate acts on behalf of another person. Advocacy is most often used when people feel disempowered—unable to function on their own behalf. Since disempowerment causes people to feel afraid to stand alone, an advocate will stand with them. The advocate will not do all the work, but only what's needed.

Abuse is an example of a terribly disempowering experience. Whether it is physical, sexual, emotional, or verbal, it has the effect of taking away a person's power and replacing it with fear. Abuse victims may need to face the abuse internally and, perhaps, even the abuser. But they may not be able to do this alone. They may need a friendly presence with them who can be with them and perhaps guide them through the more difficult parts.

Advocacy falls near the end of the continuum that represents the least amount

Personal-Power Continuum

Least Power of Choice				Most Power of Choice
REFERRAL	ADVOCACY	MEDIATION	EMPOWERMENT	ENCOURAGEMENT

of personal choice because an advocate often takes an active, directive role in resolving the person's problem.

Many youth workers and ministers get hooked on being advocates. This is a dangerous addiction because it gratifies the desire to have power and influence in people's lives. To avoid this addiction, constantly work at giving people the most power of choice. Even if you have to take the advocate's role initially, focus on quickly empowering people to act for themselves.

MEDIATION

Mediation allows more power of choice than advocacy because it calls for us to stand with people without making any decisions for them. As a mediator we may help people hear and understand other perspectives. We may also help people articulate their perspectives so they can be heard. As mediators we offer suggestions, but we do not make choices for people. Nor do we take any action on their behalf. Through mediation we may help people be reconciled to themselves, to God, to their situations, or to other people.

Mediation is very similar to a decision-making process. Mediators help brainstorm ideas, explore options for resolution, and allow choices to be made. As a mediator, you become a supportive, neutral presence as people make choices and take actions to resolve their problems.

EMPOWERMENT

The image of a coach comes to mind when we think about supporting people through empowerment. Like a coach, you may need to teach people the skills for playing the game. You can't give them natural ability, and you can't play the game for them. But you can give them the basic skills they need to get their lives under control.

As people gain these skills, they gain confidence in their ability to succeed. Sometimes people need to be taught how to go about dealing with a problem through the acquisition of parenting skills, social skills, communication skills, relationship skills, or even spiritual skills.

Once a person has acquired the skills to succeed, he or she may need permission to put them to work. This permission to succeed brings us to the final category of support on the personal-power continuum.

ENCOURAGEMENT

Cheer leading is a good metaphor for encouragement just as coaching is a good metaphor for empowerment. Sometimes people understand their problems, know what they need to do to resolve them, and even have action plans worked out. Everything is ready. All they need is someone to cheer them on to success.

Webster's New World Dictionary offers "hearten" (to give heart to) as a synonym for "encourage." We've met many people who simply lack the heart to live their lives successfully. When we become cheerleaders, we encourage people to take the first steps toward accomplishing their goals.

We always play the role of encourager from the sidelines. While we have permission to shout ideas and suggestions, we refrain because we know the person lacks nothing except the courage to move ahead. Instead, we yell, "Go for it!" to get the person going and "Hooray!" when the person makes a positive move.

Never miss an opportunity to cheer when people attempt to resolve their problems.

Cheering an attempt is more important than congratulations when the problem is resolved because, for some, success is a matter of simply trying.

Whether the attempt results in failure or success, our cheers will foster hope for the future.

When we participate in the ministry of caring as a way of helping people, we give answers of hope by listening to the person's story, facilitating decision making, and providing the support of referral, advocacy, mediation, empowerment, and encouragement. But for all our good intentions, this ministry can result in more hurt than healing if we don't conduct it wisely and carefully. For this reason we'll devote the last part of this section to a brief discussion of legal and ethical issues in helping relationships.

A Final Word:
THE LAW, ETHICS, AND YOU

At one time it was enough for those who provided counseling in a church context to have a caring heart, the wisdom of experience, and a reputation for trustworthiness. But in recent years the courts have begun to require greater accountability. Legal forecasters predict more restrictions and increased scrutiny in the future.

Why?

In some respects, we in the church have only ourselves to blame. We have not always required our ministers and workers to be adequately prepared as counselors or clearly accountable for their work. As a result, there have been abuses that have resulted in scandal, broken lives, even death. For better or worse, these abuses have drawn the full gaze of the public eye and the scrutiny of our legal system.

There are two main trouble areas, both of which require the counseling minster's utmost attention: confidentiality and sexual conduct.

Regarding confidentiality, adherence to a simple rule covers most cases.

Assume all information received in a counseling situation to be confidential unless it reveals an imminent danger to the counselee or another person.

The knowledge of physical or sexual abuse, threats of suicide, or harm to another person should *never* be kept confidential. You need to be prepared to share this information with the proper authorities—human services or police—who can offer appropriate intervention.

The second crucial issue is sexual conduct. Over the years we've served in the church, we've known many associates and some friends who have fallen victim to the sexual temptations that present themselves in close, helping relationships. Emotional intimacy and vulnerability are often a natural result of a counseling relationship. This intimacy can easily be misconstrued by some as a romantic attachment.

Unless a counseling minister is deeply committed to the highest ethical behavior, the temptation to allow a counselee to pursue a perceived romantic attachment can be overwhelming.

In the worst-case scenario, some church workers we've known have even manipulated people's confusion for their own sexual purposes.

We believe the legal and ethical issues of providing a counseling-type ministry in the church demand your careful attention. For further study, we recommend *Excellence and Ethics in Christian Counseling*, volume 30 of the Resources for Christian Counseling series published by Word, Inc. This book is wholly devoted to the legal and ethical issues confronting counseling ministers today. We strongly recommend to you the third chapter of the book, "Liability in Christian Counseling: Welcome to the Grave New World," written by George Ohlschlager.

The foundation of a successful ministry is only as strong as the integrity of the minister. Making integrity our goal and seeking to live it out in our daily lives will have a powerful, positive impact on how we perform the ministry of consolation.

Integrity will prevent us from fooling ourselves into thinking we are invulnerable to the same kinds of power trips, mind games, and indiscretions that have brought down so many others. Integrity will spur us to honesty about our credentials and the level of our expertise and training. Integrity will motivate us to set up systems of accountability for our lives and ministry. Integrity will compel us to act in the best interest of the people seeking our help.

Integrity will move us to measure all of our interventions and efforts on behalf of people by this timeless standard: What would Jesus do?

When we make integrity our goal, we won't have quarrels with any legal or ethical standards which are imposed upon us, for we will have already been subject to a higher personal code.

Part Two:
INSIGHTS AND HELPSHEETS

The Ministry of Caring in Practice

In your counseling relationships, you'll use the skills explained in the first section: listening, decision making, and support. Think of these skills as tools to be used in concert, not necessarily in any particular sequence. You'll put them to use according to the need of the moment.

Let's examine how the skills of listening, decision making, and support intertwine when an imaginary student named Mike comes to you seeking help. You'll offer emotional *support* as you *listen* to Mike tell the story of his rocky relationship with his stepfather. You'll guide Mike as he *makes decisions* about his next step. Then you may *listen* as Mike works through the possible consequences of the actions he's decided to take. Mike may need to be *supported* by your presence during a confrontation with his stepfather or by your *referral* to a professional if you feel the confrontation might become violent. Wisely combining the three basic skills, you'll help Mike reach a positive resolution to his problem.

In all your helping relationships, you'll provide the type of support that helps people retain the most power of choice. In the first section we identified five levels of support on the Personal-Power Continuum. (See the chart below.)

Determining which level of support to offer isn't always easy. Therefore, as we approach each problem in this section we'll recommend a starting point on the Personal-Power Continuum. We say "starting point" because, as you will remember, your role is to help people attain a healthier view of themselves and a greater feeling of power and responsibility in their lives. Your ultimate goal in each counseling relationship is to be an encourager who enables people to make choices based on their best understanding of themselves and their relationship with God.

For each problem we address, you'll find an Insights page with specific information for you and a photocopiable Helpsheet to hand to the person who comes to you for help. (Most of the helpsheets are designed for teenagers, but some, like the "AD(H)D" helpsheet, are for parents.) These tools will help you work together to clarify the problem, develop plans to address it, and identify the level of support you'll provide.

Personal-Power Continuum

Least Power of Choice				Most Power of Choice
REFERRAL	ADVOCACY	MEDIATION	EMPOWERMENT	ENCOURAGEMENT

1. *Insights:*
Adolescent Rebellion

What to Look For   Rebellion against parents during adolescence is a natural and expected part of growing up. It is this rebellion that strengthens the child to become an adult. Rebellion becomes a problem when it becomes so intense that personal, legal, or educational problems appear. If that happens, refer to the "Breaking the Law," "School," or "Substance Abuse" helpsheet.

What to Say   Nothing—at least to the teenager. You will see the problem intensify if you speak to the teenager on behalf of the parent. Power struggles between child and parent signal important, necessary changes in the relationship. At this time more than any other, both parties need to know how to communicate with the other. If you put yourself between them, you prevent the experience they most need to have.

What to Expect   Relief from the student; frustration, maybe even anger, from the parent. Your refusal to become the parents' representative may put a strain on your relationship with them.

How to Respond   In a joint meeting with the parent or parents and child, share these thoughts:
- Stress and struggle between parent and child during adolescence is a normal part of preparing family members to establish separate adult lives.
- As a child moves through adolescence, he or she feels the need for increasingly greater independence. The more parents try to retain control, the harder the child will push away.
- Wise parents consciously lay down their authority to control and learn to influence rather than demand.
- It's crucial that parents work at establishing communication with their child and show a willingness to renegotiate the rules of their relationship. Express your willingness to mediate, but insist that the parent and child do the work that needs to be done.

How Not to Respond   • Never put yourself between the parent and child by agreeing to talk to the child on the parent's behalf.
- Try not to overreact to what you hear about the nature of the rebellion. You need to remain calm in the midst of this family storm.

How to Follow Up   Encourage the family by assuring all members that it's typical for adolescents to seek independence. Empower family members by teaching them how to talk with and listen to each other. The message they need to be able to communicate is this: "No matter how many things change between us, one thing remains the same—my love for you." You may want to suggest working through the "Anger" helpsheet.

If rebellion results in violence or legal, school, gang, or drug and alcohol problems, refer the family for professional assistance. You may also suggest referral if either the parent or child is not willing to accept your role as mediator, but wants to put the burden of solving the problem on you.

Helpsheet 1.

1. *(Parent)* What do you remember about yourself at the age your child is now?

2. *(Parent)* How did you let your parents know that you didn't need to be dependent on them anymore?

3. *(Teenager)* How is your "declaration of independence" similar to your parent's struggle for freedom from your grandparents?

4. *(Teenager)* How is it different?

5. *(Teenager)* What is it about your struggle for independence that you think worries your parents?

6. *(Parent)* What do you see in your child's behavior that worries you?

7. *(Parent and Teenager)* Use this outline to get your relationship on a better track.

   a) Identify your goals. How will you know when things are better between you? What will be different about your feelings toward each other?
   b) When was the last time you felt these positive feelings toward each other? What were you doing differently at that time to make your relationship work?
   c) What are you willing to do now to experience those feelings again?
   d) What will you do in the coming week to build the kind of relationship you want with each other?
   e) When will we meet again to discuss difficulties and celebrate your successes?

This Week

Read the following Scriptures. Make notes about what they mean to you at this time in your life. Plan to share your notes at our next meeting.
Proverbs 22:6; Romans 8:35-39; Hebrews 13:5b-6.

2. Insights: Anger

What to Look For	Feeling anger is a human characteristic. But Christians are often taught that anger is not compatible with their faith. So we "stuff" our anger inside. That doesn't mean it goes it away. It simply finds another way out. When anger isn't expressed appropriately, it will come out as • a slow boil—glaring silence, a red face, tight lips;	• passive anger—a sweet smile and apparent agreement followed by defiant, oppositional behavior; • the silent treatment; • sniping sarcasm and criticism—instead of letting you have it all at once, you get it little by little; and • eruption—usually follows the silent treatment.

What to Say	"I've noticed that when you get angry you seem to..." (Describe behavior.) "I'm concerned that you hurt yourself and others when you do this.	Would you like to talk about how you handle anger and find some better ways to express it?"

What to Expect	"WHAT?!?!?" The person could get angry. Or you might hear, "Thanks, I would appreciate that." In	most cases, we believe this would be the response to expect.

How to Respond	If the person gets angry and it seems safe to you, use this as a teachable moment to illustrate your concern. "I understand you feel offended by my offer. Your reaction to it is how I've seen you handle your anger before. And that's what concerns me. Would you like to talk about it now?"	If the person continues to refuse, end the conversation. "It's too bad my invitation has upset you so. This doesn't seem to be a good time. Please let me know if and when you'd like to talk about it." If the person is open to working on handling anger, use the exercises on Helpsheet 2 as a guide.

How Not to Respond	• Never respond to anger with anger. It will usually cause an escalation of angry feelings and ultimately defeat your attempt to help. • Don't sermonize about the evils of	anger. Most people already know that venting anger in unhealthy ways is not the best choice. But to avoid doing that, they need to learn how to choose other options.

How to Follow Up	You can empower people to express anger in a healthy way by helping them • be aware of when they tend to get angry, • identify the feelings underlying their anger, and • develop new strategies for expressing their feelings. You can encourage them by cheering their attempts to deal differently with their anger and celebrate their victories over old patterns.	It is important to note that anger is usually the first emotion people can identify. It seems to be the one that is right on the surface for most of us. When people look below the anger, they often discover other, even more powerful feelings such as • embarrassment, • shame, • fear, • frustration, • anxiety, and • hurt.

Helpsheet 2.

(for teenagers)

1. When we get angry, there are usually physical, emotional, and mental changes that warn us that an "anger overload" is starting. Think about the last time you felt angry. What warnings of an "anger overload" can you remember?
PHYSICAL: **MENTAL:**   **EMOTIONAL:**

2. We can often slow down our anger if we act as soon as we see the warning signs. How quickly did your anger take over after the warnings? What could you do to slow down your anger response?

3. Anger is usually the first emotion that flies out of us, but it's not always the only emotion we feel. Think about the last time you were angry. What else can you remember feeling besides anger?

4. There is a five-step process we can use for expressing our anger and other feelings.

STEP 1. Be aware of when you are getting angry. ("My stomach is getting tight, my head is pounding, and I'm beginning to think hateful thoughts.")

STEP 2. Ask yourself, "What is it about this situation that is bothering me?" ("I worked for two hours on this banner, and no one has said thanks, but everyone is saying what I could have done differently.")

STEP 3. Ask yourself, "What other feelings do I have besides anger?" ("Well, I feel taken for granted, hurt, and criticized.")

STEP 4. Using "I" statements to own your feelings, share your feelings with the people who need to know them. Let them know three things: what you are feeling, why you feel as you do, and what you want to be different. ("Look, I'm feeling hurt and criticized by your comments right now, especially since no one has thanked me for my work. It makes me feel angry and want to walk out on you guys. While helpful criticism is appreciated, I think I deserve better treatment than this.")

STEP 5. Let it go and give it to God. Once you've expressed your feelings, it will do you no good to hold onto them. This is especially true if others don't acknowledge their part in the problem. If you can't let go at these times, you will be the loser because it will eat away at *you*, not others.

5. Ask a partner to work with you. Think again about the last time you were angry. Use the five-step process in that situation. Pretend your partner is responsible for the situation and practice sharing your feelings with him or her.

This Week

Many psalms written by David express his anger and frustration with other people, sometimes even with God. Read Psalm 26 and Psalm 43 and think of them the next time you feel angry. Perhaps you'd like to write your own psalm of anger.

3. Insights:
Attention Deficit (Hyperactivity) Disorder, AD(H)D

What to Look For   AD(H)D is a common disorder that you're likely to encounter in your ministry. We're going to assume for this helpsheet that a student has already been diagnosed and is in appropriate treatment. Kids with AD(H)D may or may not be hyperactive. You may see any combination of the following behaviors:

- varying degrees of inattention,
- hyperactivity,
- going from task to task without completing any of them,
- an inability to follow instructions,
- difficulty following rules of games,
- butting in line or interrupting others who are talking,
- impulsiveness, and
- boredom or distractability.

What to Say   In cases of AD(H)D we recommend that you ask the parents how you can help. If the student is in treatment, the parents may be able to give you specific instructions on how to deal with him or her. Let the parents know that you will be willing to work with them and offer feedback regarding their child's behavior and progress in your youth program.

What to Expect   Kids with AD(H)D are often on medication. In some cases the medication is used only during school or during the week. If this is the case, the student may have difficulty at youth group. You may need to discuss with parents the possibility of the student taking medication before church activities. Parents of AD(H)D children are usually open to receiving as much support as possible. The key is to be positive and encouraging.

How to Respond   Assure parents of your interest and support. Ask if they have literature about AD(H)D they could share with you. If you find information the parents may not have, share it with them. Emphasize the student's positive characteristics. Parents of kids with AD(H)D seldom hear good things and are often overwhelmed with the negative aspects of their children's behavior.

How Not to Respond
- Be careful not to contradict the recommendations of those providing treatment.
- Try not to focus on the negative behavior or blame the student for behavior that is out of his or her control.
- Don't overlook or excuse behavior the student can control. (Communication with parents is important to discern the difference between behavior that is controllable and behavior the student has little control over.)
- Try not to single the student out because of his or her behavior problems.

How to Follow Up   When a student is having a difficult time with his or her behavior, take the student aside and say: "I know you're having a tough time controlling things tonight. Let's take a short break, then come back to this activity later." Forcing a confrontation may cause the student to become more defiant. If you adjust your activities to avoid confrontation, you'll find the student more responsive.

Proper medication and treatment may dramatically decrease negative behavior. Some kids are more responsive to treatment than others. Your level of support and encouragement will depend on the effectiveness of treatment.

For further information on referral, check out "Attention Deficit (Hyperactivity) Disorder, AD(H)D" in Part Three.

1. Are you currently involved in counseling or support groups with your teenager?

2. Is your teenager on medication? Will he or she be taking the medication prior to coming to church and youth group?

3. What are your teenager's strengths? What does he or she enjoy doing?

4. What behavior do I need to be aware of?

5. How can I be of help to you and your teenager?

6. Would you like occasional feedback regarding how your child is getting along in church activities?

This Week

Reflect on the concepts of patience and endurance found in Romans 15:4-5. Be aware that there are people here at church who care about your family and are committed to praying for and supporting your child.

4. Insights:
Body Image and Puberty

What to Look For

"Am I normal?" Nearly every adolescent wrestles with this question. Kids often confront the problems of puberty in silence and are left to draw their own conclusions. Puberty is not only a time of tremendous change for kids, it is also the time when many people form their most enduring physical images of themselves. The kids most likely to need your help are those who

- are early bloomers;
- are late bloomers;
- acquire prominent adult physical characteristics so quickly that they stand out among their friends (the dark-bearded boy or the full-chested girl, for example); and
- those who dramatically change physically but remain remarkably unchanged emotionally.

When kids approach you, they may not be aware that they are feeling as they do because of the changes of puberty. Therefore, you may need to steer the conversation to that topic.

What to Say

"You seem to have changed so much in just a few months. I wonder if that has anything to do with what you're feeling. What do you think?"

What to Expect

Expect a willingness to pursue the conversation. Or the student might ask, "What do you mean?" This allows you to introduce the subject of puberty and explain how it might trigger some of the feelings he or she has expressed.

How to Respond

Share the following information:

- Puberty is a time of rapid physical, emotional, social, and sexual development that everyone goes through on the road to adulthood. It can take anywhere from a few months to a couple of years or more.
- The changes of puberty can be kind of scary and confusing because it feels like we've lost control of our bodies and our emotions.
- Some of the best things you can do for yourself are to
  a) remain calm,
  b) learn more about puberty by reading and talking to people who can give you good information, and
  c) talk with a trusted friend about your feelings and experiences.

How Not to Respond

- Don't make light of kids' feelings. Though *you* know what's going on and that they'll survive, kids don't have that perspective.
- Avoid overloading them with information. Kids may not be looking for a complete lecture on sexuality.
- Don't fake it. If you're unsure about an answer to a student's question, say, "I don't know," then offer to do some research.
- Avoid discussing a student's questions about puberty in public.

How to Follow Up

Stay in touch with the student through private, informal conversations. Your encouragement through genuine caring and empowerment through education are very important. A rough passage through puberty may adversely affect a student's self-esteem and body image for years to come. Negative self-esteem and poor body image are two factors that put kids at risk for involvement in premature sexual activity, drug and alcohol abuse, and influence by a negative peer group.

Consider reading these excellent books on puberty: *Preparing for Adolescence* by James Dobson (Tyndale); *What's Happening to My Body? Book for Boys* edited by Lynda Madaras and Dane Saavedra (Newmarket Press); and *What's Happening to My Body? Book for Girls* edited by Lynda Madaras and Area Madaras (Newmarket Press).

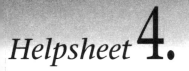

Helpsheet 4.

1. Which statement best describes how you're feeling right now?

    a) This is cool! I'm finally beginning to look like an adult!
    b) I feel so different. Other kids tease me because my body is growing faster (or not as fast) as theirs.
    c) I wish this weren't happening. It can be so embarrassing!
    d) Sometimes I wonder if there is something wrong with me.

2. What do you like best about all the changes?

3. What do you like least about these changes?

4. What would you like to know more about or understand better?

5. What could I do to help you right now?

This Week

Luke 2:52 illustrates four dimensions of human life. Just as Jesus grew mentally, physically, socially, and spiritually through his adolescence, so will you. Take a few minutes this week to jot down some ways you've been growing in each of these dimensions.

5. Insights: Breaking the Law

What to Look For
Kids involved in illegal activities will not be highly visible to you. Most of what you do see, such as avoidance of church activities or leaving a positive peer group for a negative one, can be interpreted as normal adolescent behavior. In short, you're not likely to know for certain that one of your kids is having trouble with the law until you read it in the newspaper or learn about it from his or her friends, parents, or the authorities.

What to Say
"I've heard from _____ that you've been having some trouble with the law. I'm worried about you. What's this all about?"

What to Expect
Generally, first-time offenders and kids who are simply acting out other problems by breaking the law are inclined to respond with shame and embarrassment. Habitual offenders and gang members may show less remorse—or too much remorse if they're adept at playing the game. Because breaking the law includes a breach of trust, don't put too much weight on the first response. While you may give the student the benefit of the doubt, reserve your judgment until you see him or her demonstrate trustworthy behavior.

How to Respond
"Fool me once, shame on you. Fool me twice, shame on me." This old saying illustrates the importance of striking a balance between good faith and good sense in dealing with kids. Good faith says you want to believe kids are above the behavior that got them into trouble, but good sense reminds you that you have hard evidence to the contrary.

Your response may be to set up a rule for your interaction that expresses the dilemma you feel: "I'm sorry for the trouble you've had. I think you can make different choices that will take care of this problem and help you avoid future ones. I'll know you can do this when I see you making these better choices. As you show me that I can trust you to make good choices, you'll see that I'll be here for you."

In most cases it's best to refer the student and parents for family counseling and possibly to an attorney.

How Not to Respond
● Avoid the extremes of believing nothing the student says or everything the student says.
● Make no promises of your unquestioning support.
● Don't punish the student. If punishment is required, let the law take care of it.

How to Follow Up
A student who's had a run-in with the law needs your encouragement and possibly your mediation. The student needs to know that while you're disappointed about what happened, you still believe in him or her. You can show this by spending time with the student and working to include him or her in your group activities. You can play a mediating role by offering a character reference when you feel comfortable doing so and by attending court proceedings.

A student involved in gang activity is at extremely high risk if efforts are made to remove him or her from the gang. A rule for many gangs is that death is the only way out. When you suspect a teen's criminal involvement is gang related, immediately consult a law-enforcement specialist with expertise in gang-membership intervention. Be prepared to provide a referral for the parents to a treatment setting where their child can receive help and possibly protection. You can get this information from your local law-enforcement authorities.

Helpsheet 5.

1. What were you hoping to get when you risked breaking the law?

2. What could you do differently now to get what you want?

3. How did your actions cause problems for
  a) your parents?

  b) law-enforcement authorities?

  c) the person or people you harmed?

  d) yourself?

4. Complete this sentence: To make right what I've done, I need to . . .

5. Complete this sentence: To regain the trust of everyone I've hurt I need to . . .

6. What could I do that would help you accomplish these things?

This Week

Read Romans 13:1-10. How does loving each other fulfill the law?
Read John 8:1-11. How do you feel about Jesus' attitude toward the woman who was caught by authorities?

6. Insights:
Breaking Up

What to Look For Strangely, the symptoms of breaking up are very similar to the symptoms of falling in love:
- obsession with the other person as shown in an inability to focus or incessant talking about the person;
- mood swings that match the ups and downs of the relationship; and
- social isolation, caused either by spending every free minute with the other person or by healing from the ending of the romance.

When you see these things happening to a student after the breakup of a romantic relationship, you'd do well to contact the student if he or she hasn't already approached you.

What to Say "I understand you and _____ have broken up. You must be feeling kind of low. Would you like to talk about it?"

What to Expect Most kids will be willing to talk about it. Don't be alarmed at a show of emotion. You should be more concerned if the student is unwilling to talk yet continues to seem obsessed, withdrawn, or moody.

How to Respond The best thing you can do is listen. Breaking up can cause teenagers to grieve for a long time. The intensity of the grief is approximately equal to the couple's level of intimacy. Kids who've been in emotionally or sexually intimate relationships will generally feel the full weight of grief. Our experience has been that an *emotionally* intimate relationship is harder to lose than a *sexually* intimate relationship.

If a student chooses not to talk to you, respect that choice but stay in touch informally. Be available when the student does want to talk.

How Not to Respond
- Don't minimize a student's grief. It's not uncommon for teenagers to become suicidal when they have lost at love. If you suspect a student might harm himself or herself or another person, inform the proper authorities and the student's parents.
- Don't try to give advice. But be willing to help the student brainstorm his or her next steps if asked.

How to Follow Up Your most important role during a breakup is to stay in touch. You'll give encouragement by listening to the student talk about his or her past love and by asking questions about that person.

1. Tell me something about your relationship with the person you broke up with. How did you meet?

2. What made your relationship special?

3. What happened to change it? When did you notice this change?

4. What do you think could have been done to avoid the ending of the relationship?

5. Ten years from now, what's the first thing you'll remember about this relationship?

6. Name three or four things you could do to help yourself get through this difficult time.
  a)
  b)
  c)
  d)

Which of these things will you do first, and when will you do it?

7. What can I do to help you through this painful time?

This Week

People may stop loving us, but God never does. Read in Romans 8:31-39 about the never-ending, everlasting, nonstop love of God through Jesus Christ.

7. Insights:
Community Crisis

What to Look For The immediate response to a community crisis or natural disaster is shock and disbelief. People may be killed, missing, or left homeless. Many private, local, and national services immediately step in to help. Assuming that you're not a direct victim, you and the kids in your youth group may find that the best way to help is to get involved with the services already in place.

After the initial crisis and shock are over, you'll need to address the emotional responses of victims and volunteers. They can have problems with
- depression,
- hopelessness,
- confusion,
- anger,
- fear, and
- emotional and physical exhaustion.

What to Say "What happened to you and your family during the flood?"

"What was it like to help clean up after the storm? What were your reactions?"

What to Expect People will want to tell about their experiences over and over again. Telling and retelling helps people make sense of what happened and process how they feel about it. They may express outrage about how systems and services failed. They may express grief over the things they lost or the people who died. Emotional healing takes a long time. Be aware of your own responses. Find someone you can share with as well. In order to be helpful to others, you'll need to work through your own issues related to the crisis.

How to Respond Listen and share. People will feel a need to support as well as to be supported. You may want to get together as a group to work through these issues. Take your time. Don't feel that your first meeting has to bring closure to the situation. Meet as many times as necessary. Involve a variety of people, including parents.

How Not to Respond • Don't minimize the trauma of those who have experienced less loss or destruction than others.

• Don't assume that the emotional stress is over once things settle into a normal routine.

How to Follow Up Utilize the civic resources that are available in the aftermath of a community crisis. Community mental-health centers, United Way agencies, the Salvation Army, and other organizations often provide support groups and counseling in the affected areas. Getting involved can put your kids in touch with the larger community, help them deal with feelings of isolation and hopelessness, and teach them that they're valued members of the community.

Families and individuals may experience more frustration later on, when financial problems occur. They may have to relocate or rebuild. If insurance doesn't cover the losses, lifestyles may be drastically altered. Your support and encouragement will be needed throughout this time.

1. What are the effects of the crisis on your family?

2. How are you directly affected?

Complete the following sentences:

3. The worst part of the crisis for me is when . . .

4. If only I could . . .

5. When I look at what happened I feel . . .

6. One thing that has helped me is . . .

7. I can really use your help dealing with . . .

This Week

Reflect on Psalm 27. What images of safety and security do you find? Record how you see and feel God's presence each day.

Insights:
8. Conduct Disorders

What to Look For   Occasionally you'll run across a student who appears to be out of control. He or she may get into legal trouble. This kind of behavior may indicate a conduct disorder. Such kids are frustrating to work with. For in-depth information, refer to "Conduct Disorders" in Part Three. The behaviors to be aware of are

- stealing,
- forgery,
- running away,
- lying,
- fire setting,
- skipping school,
- breaking and entering,
- destroying property,
- cruelty to animals,
- rape or sexual molestation,
- robbery, and
- fighting with or without weapons.[1]

What to Say   "You've been getting into a lot of trouble lately, and you seem frustrated. Would you be willing to get together to talk about some of these things?"

What to Expect   You may find the student who's just stepped into his or her first big problem is willing to talk. He or she may be feeling afraid and alone. More often, however, students with conduct disorders are angry and have little respect for authority. You may represent that authority and be rejected. Kids may blame everyone else for their problems and behavior without taking responsibility for themselves. Students with conduct disorders may be in your youth group by parental force and may test your authority by acting rude, obnoxious, threatening, or defiant.

How to Respond   If the student tests your authority, avoid losing control and responding in anger. Most adults are already angry with this teenager. Stand firm in retaining the expectations for your group and confront the student individually with your concerns. The key for youth workers is *not to give up,* as the the student will expect you to do. These kids have a high need for acceptance. You'll be more effective if they feel you accept them regardless of their behavior and faults.

How Not to Respond
- Don't respond angrily even if you're angry. Say what makes you angry, but do so in a calm and controlled manner.
- Don't avoid working with the student, even though it's difficult and the immediate rewards are few.
- Don't allow the student to disrupt group activities without consequences or confrontation.

How to Follow Up   Kids who seem out of control are attempting to gain control. If you provide consistent support and avoid reacting out of anger, you're likely to communicate to these students that they're important and appreciated. You may also be setting a good example for parents who are probably frustrated and tired of dealing with the problem. Too often, the families of adolescents with conduct disorders have given up or continue to react in ways that don't work and may, in fact, reinforce defiant behavior. Check in with parents and offer to support them as well. The student may need your help in communicating frustrations, anger, and fears to parents. Here your roles would be mediation, advocacy, empowerment, and encouragement.

Helpsheet 8.

Complete the following sentences:

1. If I were to describe myself I would say I am ...

2. The worst trouble I've gotten into is ...

3. What scares me the most about the things I've done is ...

4. I'm most angry at _____ because ...

5. When I do things that get me into trouble I feel ...

6. The trouble with my parents is that they ...

7. If I could change three things about me and my life, I would change
   a)

   b)

   c)

This Week

Read Galatians 5:13-15. Who is your behavior hurting? What would you like to be free from?

9. Insights: Death and Loss

What to Look For

The loss of someone close to a teenager through death, divorce, or even moving can be traumatic. Grief is a strong emotion; it's both necessary and normal. Sometimes an intense grief response goes beyond what's considered normal. In that case, the student needs professional help. We'll address normal reactions here; we recommend that you refer kids who demonstrate more intense responses to a professional mental-health worker.

Typical responses to death or loss are
- depression,
- decrease in appetite,
- weight loss,
- crying spells,
- difficulty sleeping,
- low energy,
- numbness,
- shock,
- loneliness, and
- guilt.

What to Say

During difficult times of loss, what you say is not nearly as important as being physically and emotionally present to offer comfort and support. If the symptoms continue for several days, encourage the student to talk about his or her feelings.

"Tell me things you have thought about since _____ died (or left)."

What to Expect

When you make this request, be prepared to listen. Kids will usually be ready to share the pain they're experiencing. They may express anger at the one who is gone, at themselves, at God, and maybe even at you. They'll find it hard to accept that the person they care for is truly gone. They may express the desire to die themselves to be with the one they've lost. Or, depending on the circumstances, they may be relieved that the person is gone. They may also feel guilty about feeling relieved.

The best way to prepare yourself is to expect a variety of responses.

How to Respond

Listen, listen, listen. There is little you can say to make grieving people feel better. Instead, allow them to use you as a sounding board. They can hear themselves and begin to work out ways to deal with their pain. It's important to let grieving people know you're available. If you hear them make irrational statements that concern you, gently ask, "Can you tell me what you mean by that?" This allows them an opportunity to rethink their positions and adjust their beliefs.

How Not to Respond

- Don't trivialize their feelings by suggesting that the one who died wouldn't want them to feel this way.
- Don't minimize their loss. For example, if a person's closest friend has moved away, don't suggest that this is "not the end of the world."
- Avoid clichés that don't address the feelings of loss, such as "He's gone to a better place."
- Don't avoid grieving people, even when it's difficult for you. Your ministry of caring is of great importance to those who are devastated or traumatized by loss.

How to Follow Up

Facing holidays, birthdays, and other special times is difficult for people who've lost someone close to them. Then comes the anniversary of the individual's death or departure. Be aware of these times and be ready to provide support and encouragement.

An excellent book on grief is *Grieving: How to Go on Living When Someone You Love Dies* by Therese A. Rando, Ph.D., (Free Press). You may also want to obtain the video *Losing Hurts...But Not Forever* by Marshmedia, Box 8020, Shawnee Mission, KS 66208.

Helpsheet 9.

1. How has your loss affected you? your family?

2. (Circle all that apply.) Since the person I cared for died (or left), I have felt

angry   depressed   lonely   relieved   dazed   frightened

other_____

3. How would you describe your relationship with that person?

4. What worries you most now?

5. What one thing have you learned about yourself through this?

6. What can I do to help you right now?

This Week

In 2 Corinthians 1:3-11 Paul describes God's compassion and comfort. He appears to be speaking from experience. Spend time considering this passage throughout the week.

10. Insights: Depression

What to Look For Feelings of depression range from mild symptoms of feeling "blue" to clinical depression accompanied by suicidal thoughts. The symptoms include

- irritability and anger,
- a change in eating habits,
- oversleeping or insomnia,
- a loss of energy,
- feelings of worthlessness,
- withdrawal from social interactions,
- a lack of interest in pleasurable activities,
- an inability to concentrate, and
- thoughts of death.

When depression disrupts normal, day-to-day functioning such as school performance and relationships at home, suggest seeking professional help. You'll find further information under "Depression" in Part Three.[2]

What to Say "I've noticed that you haven't seemed happy for quite a while. I know this is a tough time for you. How have you been handling it?"

What to Expect This statement lets the student know that you're aware of his or her problem. It also requires a response beyond yes or no. You may find the adolescent ready to talk. He or she may express anger and perhaps direct it at you. Don't take it personally. It's likely that the student is merely venting and isn't really angry with you.

How to Respond Be ready to listen to what the student says, as well as what he or she doesn't say. Be slow to offer advice and quick to offer support. Help the student identify negative self-talk and work at developing and using only positive statements. Provide positive reinforcement when the student has made progress—you may have to start with small successes at first.

How Not to Respond

- Don't pressure kids to talk. Let them know you'll be available whenever they're ready.
- Avoid "quick fix" advice. The reasons for depression are often complex. Kids may feel even more hopeless when quick fixes are unsuccessful.
- Don't minimize the importance of their problems. That response leads kids to believe that no one understands them.

How to Follow Up A depressed person often lacks motivation. You may be tempted to step in and do things for depressed kids that they need to do for themselves. Avoid this temptation. Instead, help kids identify the things they need to do. Then develop a plan that's divided into small units so it doesn't overwhelm the individual. Accomplishing small tasks allows kids to regain control of their lives.

Many depressed adolescents suffer from feelings of low self-worth. The depressed adolescent may need encouragement from a variety of outside sources such as family, peers, teachers, and you. As the feelings of depression diminish, the student regains a sense of self-worth through the satisfaction of completing tasks, performing well, and having positive relationships. Until then, your role as an encourager is important as you help the student identify success and progress.

Helpsheet 10.

Complete the following sentences:

1. The thing that's most on my mind is . . .

2. If only _____ would change, I would feel better because . . .

3. I'm most angry at . . .

4. I first noticed I was depressed when . . .

5. My level of depression or sadness right now is

none			somewhat depressed					very depressed	
1	2	3	4	5	6	7	8	9	10

6. In one month, I would like my level of depression or sadness to be

none			somewhat depressed					very depressed	
1	2	3	4	5	6	7	8	9	10

This Week

Read Psalm 42. How are your feelings like the feelings King David expresses in this psalm? What hope did King David find? Where can you find hope?

11. *Insights:* Domestic Violence

What to Look For   Domestic violence is an ugly fact of life. In most cases, the violence is committed by husbands against wives. A high percentage of cases involve alcohol. The effect of domestic violence on children is tremendous. You'll find a variety of responses from adolescents, including

- a fear of a parent or parents,
- extreme anxiety,
- a drop in school performance,
- aggressive behavior,
- low self-worth,
- running away from home,
- depression,
- behavior problems,
- a withdrawal from social situations, and
- difficulty in developing relationships.

What to Say   "I know that things at home are pretty rough for you right now. How are you holding up?"

What to Expect   Relief that someone is interested in helping. Realizing that the secret is out may bring fear of what will happen next. Or, there may be denial that any problems exist.

How to Respond   In cases of domestic violence, the adolescent needs to be supported and feel that he or she has a friend and advocate. You may not be able to fix the problem at home, but you will be able to provide a place for the teenager to turn when it happens again.

How Not to Respond

- Don't suggest that the teenager can do anything about the violence or the alcohol problem.
- Don't encourage kids to try to be peacemakers.
- Don't make excuses for the student's behavior. Kids need to take responsibility for their own actions.

How to Follow Up   If violence continues, help the teenager develop a plan for when it happens again. The plan could include

- going to a safe place,
- calling you or the police,
- making arrangements beforehand to stay with a relative or friend, or
- asking the police to remove the children or one parent from the home.

Share with the parents your concern about the effects of violence on their child. Give the victim the telephone number of the local domestic-violence hot line and the name and phone number of a qualified therapist.

Be the teenager's advocate and encourager. You may be the only one providing support for him or her. Until things change for the better, your role is extremely important.

1. What are you afraid will happen when people at your house argue?

2. Why are you afraid?

3. What do you do when they physically hurt each other?

4. How do you feel when they fight?

5. What steps can you take if and when they become violent again?
   a)
   b)
   c)
   d)

6. How would you like me to help you during this time?

This Week

Read Psalm 77. How has God helped you in your day of trouble? Write out your feelings as David did in this psalm.

12. Insights: Eating Disorders

What to Look For
During adolescence, kids are especially sensitive about their appearance and about criticism from their peers. More females than males develop eating disorders. She will typically be a high achiever from a highly structured family with one or both parents exercising extreme control over the children. Anorexia nervosa and bulimia nervosa are two common eating disorders. In many cases the symptoms overlap. The symptoms to be aware of are

ANOREXIA NERVOSA
- refusal to maintain normal body weight,
- failure to make expected weight gains during growth periods,
- fear of becoming fat,
- feeling fat or overweight even when underweight, and
- absence of three consecutive menstrual cycles.

BULIMIA NERVOSA
- binge eating;
- self-induced vomiting;
- feelings of a lack of self-control related to eating; and
- use of laxatives, fasting, or excessive exercise in attempts to lose weight.[3]

What to Say
Initially, say nothing to the teenager. She'll usually deny that there are any problems. Given the severity of eating disorders and the potential for physical problems, we recommend that you share your concerns with the adolescent's parents. Report suspicious behavior you have observed or heard from other kids. Recommend that the parents and adolescent meet with a physician.

If the student has been diagnosed and is in treatment, wait for her to approach you. Even if she's reluctant to talk about the eating disorder, you may still be able to provide encouragement.

What to Expect
You may encounter denial and disbelief from the parents. Once the teen becomes aware of your concerns, she may express anger toward you. You are revealing a well-guarded secret and forcing her to confront herself and her parents. If a diagnosis is made and the family enters treatment, she may express tremendous relief that the secret is finally out.

How to Respond
Share with the parents a complete description of the symptoms you've observed. Give information about mental-health counseling. If parents are angry because you've brought the problem into the open, explain that the seriousness of the symptoms made that your only option. Let them know that you'll be available to support them.

How Not to Respond
- Don't confront the family with accusations. Instead, present your concerns with compassion.
- Don't attempt to identify and confront the family-relationship issues. These are best dealt with by mental-health professionals.

How to Follow Up
Your ministry is one of referral and encouragement. After helping with a referral, you may not receive any more feedback. However, you can continue to provide encouragement without broaching the subject of eating disorders. In fact, we feel that it's best not to inquire about treatment. You can continue to reinforce the student's self-worth and encourage her to be involved with the youth group.

(for parents)

1. Have you noticed any changes in your daughter's behavior over the past several weeks or months?

2. How well do you think your daughter is handling her various responsibilities?

3. When you were her age, what responsibilities did you have? How were they different from or similar to your daughter's?

4. When you were overwhelmed as a teenager, how did you deal with it?

5. Are you willing to meet with a therapist to discuss how you can modify your home environment to help your daughter?

- -

(for teenagers)

1. How would you describe yourself to someone you've never met?

2. What are your strengths and weaknesses?

3. How are they different from other teenagers'? How are they the same?

4. What can I do to help you?

This Week

Second Peter 1:3-11 says that God has given us everything we need to serve him. List the good qualities God has given you. Write two or three ways you can develop each of these qualities.

13. Insights: Failure

What to Look For — Our society celebrates success. We're rewarded internally and externally when we succeed. Kids' successes are examined in school, on the playing field, in the arts, in relationships, and even in our churches. When kids fail to meet the expectations of their peers, parents, teachers, coaches, and even themselves, they may be in for a major letdown.

Teenagers can be very hard on themselves. They may experience

- low self-worth,
- depression,
- isolation,
- low motivation,
- ridicule,
- anger toward others and themselves, and
- fear of taking risks in the future.

What to Say — "You seem to be upset about your performance in _____. How are you taking it?"

What to Expect — Kids will probably talk about how badly they performed and what people said to them. They may even say they will never try again.

How to Respond — Let kids vent their feelings at first. Listen carefully to what they say about themselves. Rephrase their negative statements about themselves in the form of questions such as "You believe you can't sing?" This allows kids to confront their irrational statements.

How Not to Respond —
- Don't argue with what they say.
- Don't reinforce untrue statements they make about themselves.
- Don't minimize how they feel about their failure.

How to Follow Up — Help kids re-examine their abilities and levels of success. Adolescents sometimes focus on one large goal without setting intermediate goals to get them there. You can help teens identify practical and attainable goals. Success at this level will increase self-worth and motivate kids to continue.

Some kids lack the abilities to succeed in certain areas. They may not have an ear for music, the coordination for sports, or the memorization skills to learn a role in a play. If kids appear to be setting themselves up for failure, confront them gently and help them set realistic expectations. They may choose a lesser role in activities they enjoy, such as a stagehand or team manager rather than trying for a starring role or a spot in the starting lineup.

1. What are you really good at?

2. What would you like to be better at?

3. Name three small goals that you can work toward to help you become better at what you named in question 2.
a)
b)
c)

4. When you feel you've performed poorly, what do you say to yourself?

5. How could you change those negative statements to helpful and affirming ones?

6. How can this experience with failure help you succeed in the future?

7. Ten years from now, what will you say you learned from this experience?

This Week

Read Matthew 26:69-75. How did Peter fail in his commitment to Jesus? How is this similar to failures you've experienced? How is it different?

Read Matthew 25:14-30. According to this parable, what is worse: failing or not trying? How are you developing your talents?

14. Insights:
Families–Blended

What to Look For   If divorce isn't complicated enough for kids, remarriage certainly can be. Blended families rarely function as well as TV's mythical, magical *Brady Bunch*. Stepparenting isn't easy, nor is it easy for children to adjust to stepparents. Success or failure is usually determined in the first few months the new family is together. You'll know the blending process isn't going well for a student if you observe or learn of

- frequent complaints about the stepparent,
- violence in the family,
- the student avoiding home or other contact with the stepparent, or
- chronic fighting between the student and other siblings or stepsiblings.

What to Say   "What's it like having _____ as your stepparent? How's your new family doing?"

What to Expect   If kids feel positive about the family, you can expect them to say so quite freely. They may speak well of family members but mention the stress of adjustment.

If kids don't feel positive about the family, you'll see it on their faces as well as in what they say.

How to Respond   If the response is positive, simply use the time to give encouragement and talk about how the adjustment process is going. If the response is negative, use the questions on the helpsheet to explore the problem and determine whether referral is needed.

How Not to Respond
- Avoid referring to the stepparent as "mom" or "dad" unless the student uses those titles. If you're unsure how to refer to the stepparent, use the person's first name or ask the student what he or she calls the stepparent.
- The least effective response from you is to preach a sermon on the value of families. Part of the difficulty may be letting go of the old family and accepting the new one as a family at all.
- Avoid making any agreements to deal with one family member on behalf of another. People need to work out their own conflicts.

How to Follow Up   Listen to kids' frustrations, fears, and hurts. Empower kids by teaching them how to open lines of communication with their parents and stepparents. Stress the importance of expressing their feelings clearly without blaming others.

If you feel communication has broken down in a blended family, refer the student and parents to a family therapist. Contact the parent and stepparent to make an appointment to discuss your concern for their child. Make sure the student knows you're making this contact. At your meeting, simply share your concern that the child is having some difficulty adjusting to the family's new situation. Give them the name and phone number of the family therapist you recommend. Assure them that you'll be available for support and encouragement as they work with the therapist.

1. How do you feel about your family? Good? Proud? Angry? Depressed? Frustrated?

2. What is it about your family that makes you feel that way?

3. How does each member make your family a good or bad place to live?

Parent—

Stepparent—

Siblings—

Stepsiblings—

You—

4. What do you think needs to happen to make your family a happy place for you and everyone else?

5. What part can you play in that process?

6. How can I help you through this adjustment period?

This Week

Read about the conflict between two sisters in Luke 10:38-42. Why do you think Jesus responded the way he did? What encouragement do you think Jesus might give to you?

15. Insights:
Families in Crisis

What to Look For A variety of things can fall into this category: house fires, severe accidents, burglary, or loss of a parent's job. Usually the initial response is shock. The family members will often run on "autopilot" to get through the initial crisis. Later, emotional problems such as these may surface:

- exhaustion,
- depression,
- feelings of hopelessness,
- crying spells,
- isolation,
- anger,
- confusion, and
- uncertainty about the future.

What to Say "I know this has been a tough time for you and your family. What's the most difficult thing to handle right now?"

What to Expect You may get a hopeless reply such as "I don't know." Or, the student might use this opportunity to let go of bottled-up feelings of grief and anger.

How to Respond Let the student know that it's OK to share feelings openly. An adolescent's life is full of uncertainties anyway. A family crisis compounds the fright and confusion. Sometimes a person who's been through a crisis needs to tell the story over and over again to make sense of it and put it into perspective.

How Not to Respond Don't try to fix the problem. Just hear the student out and offer support. Kids need to know they're not alone in this crisis.

How to Follow Up It's helpful to gather a support group for kids in crisis. Members of the youth group are a good resource. Find as many ways as possible to show your support and sense of community. Help the family with cleanup. Go shopping for clothes with the adolescent. Take the family out to eat or make a meal to be shared by the family and support group. Always be available to listen and encourage.

As you can see, the follow-up in times of crisis can take on various forms. Brainstorm with the support group creative ways to help. Kids in the support group will also gain a lot from such an experience.

You'll need to spend some individual time with the teenager to address his or her specific needs that may not involve the rest of the family.

Helpsheet 15.

1. Now that the worst is over, how are you and your family doing?

2. What was the most difficult thing for you to deal with?

3. What did you do to get through the worst of the crisis?

4. What's going to be the most difficult thing for you to deal with in the next few days or weeks?

5. How can I help you?

6. How can the youth group help you?

This Week

Read Psalm 27 throughout this week. Choose two or three verses that have special meaning to you. Write them on slips of paper and place them where you'll see them often—in your wallet, on your mirror, or on the lamp beside your bed.

16. Insights:
Families–Disabled and Challenged

What to Look For Sometime in your work with teenagers, you're likely to run across families with mentally or physically disabled or challenged people. All members of challenged families may experience frustration around the same issue—access. Gaining access to the variety of experiences enjoyed by every other member of our society is a major difficulty for nearly all challenged families, affecting their opportunities to
- freely participate in activities,
- advance in careers,
- develop loving relationships, and
- obtain educations.

What to Say "How's your family? How is it going at home?"

What to Expect A common mistake is to assume that members of a challenged family *feel* different because we see them as different. If we expect them to act according to our perceptions, we're treating them unjustly. Their problems will be essentially the same as the problems of any other family, with the addition of access issues. In this regard you might hear the student talk about the frustration of dealing with obstacles to doing what he or she would like.

How to Respond Listen empathically. To help yourself understand a student's feelings, you might say, "I've never experienced life exactly as you know it, so I don't fully understand all the challenges you face. Can you talk to me about some of those challenges and how you're trying to overcome them?"

How Not to Respond ● Be careful not to patronize challenged people or families by trying to compensate for the "handicap" you perceive. Examples might be speaking too loudly to a deaf person or rushing to offer assistance to someone in a wheelchair. Don't assume that you know how to respond. It's far better to ask.
● Avoid the use of the terms "abnormal," "disabled," or "handicapped."

How to Follow Up You can become an encourager and advocate for challenged families in your church. They need to be encouraged to continue their struggle to get full and equal access to all they wish to do. Encourage your church and youth group to actively plan for the involvement of all members. This may mean making changes in programming and in the location of activities.

You might create a corps of volunteers to provide transportation, physical assistance, respite care, or anything else that could help a challenged family to become more fully involved in church life. You may need to brief your group about common attitudes that unintentionally exclude challenged families.

1. What can you tell me to help me understand what it's like to live in your family?

2. How are you feeling about your involvement in the church or group?
a) Great!
b) It's OK.
c) Not so good.

Tell me why you feel the way you do.

3. Is there anything that makes it difficult for you to be involved in our church or our youth group? If so, what is it?

4. What do you need to feel more involved in the church or group?

5. How can I help you feel more accepted and involved in the church or group?

This Week

Read Acts 2:1-11. What does this passage tell you about how much God wants everyone to have access to the gospel of Jesus Christ?

17. Insights: Families–Divorce

What to Look For   Watching their parents' marriage deteriorate can be more emotionally devastating for kids than the final results of divorce. Why is this? There's a great deal of conflict and anxiety among family members as everyone waits for decisions and settlements to be made. Kids experiencing the divorce of their parents often ride an emotional roller coaster as they fluctuate between the real (a bad marriage) and the ideal (wanting an intact family). Kids may express feelings they can't verbalize through

- an inability to concentrate,
- moodiness,
- acting out,
- trouble with the law,
- poor grades, or
- social withdrawal.

What to Say   "Since learning about your folks' divorce I've been thinking about you. I often wonder how you're doing. How is it going for you?"

What to Expect   "It's going OK," "I'm fine," and other statements of silence. The fluctuation between the real and the ideal may make students unwilling or unable to talk about their feelings during the divorce process. Their silence is a means of denying that the divorce is happening. In the "magical thinking" of adolescents, kids may fear that talking about the process will only hasten it. Already feeling responsible for the breakup of their parents' marriage (this is an almost universal feeling among children of divorcing parents), they cannot bear to risk confirming that terrible belief.

How to Respond   If kids choose to remain silent, let them have their silence and their space. It is easier to understand their behavior when we remember that these kids are grieving. And like all grieving people, they're moving toward acceptance of the difficult changes in their families. Respect their right to talk to you in their own time. At least they know you care.

If they respond to you, use the questions on Helpsheet 17 to continue the conversation.

How Not to Respond   Avoid siding with one parent over another. The student may already be feeling pressured to choose between them. It won't help the teenager feel less pressured and you won't be a safe person to talk to if the student knows you've taken sides.

How to Follow Up   Be prepared to give support and encouragement to children of divorcing families. Unless a student chooses to let you into his or her falling-apart world, much of your work will be done behind the scenes. You can be an encourager by hanging out with the student and staying in frequent, informal contact. Don't talk about the changes in the student's family unless he or she brings it up. Your supportive presence conveys a powerful message: "I'm here and I care."

If you suspect at any time that the student is depressed, be ready to make a referral. See "Depression" in Part Three for information about steps to take if the student has become depressed.

Complete the following sentences:

1. The toughest thing about my folks' divorce is...

2. The best thing about my folks' divorce is...

3. The way I'm feeling about the divorce right now is

Poor				OK					Good
1	2	3	4	5	6	7	8	9	10

4. One thing I've learned about myself since the divorce started is...

5. No matter what happens with my parents, these three things will always be true:
a)

b)

c)

6. You can help me during this divorce by...

This Week

Read Psalm 63:1-8. What comforting thoughts do you find? In what ways has God "supported you with his right hand"?

18. Insights: Families–Foster

What to Look For   Foster families present several challenges to you as a youth minister. Some families keep adolescents only for a short time. Others are committed to long-term foster care, which may mean the adolescent will be staying until young adulthood. Some foster parents are licensed to provide care for a specific child such as a relative or the child of a friend.

● Foster children inevitably carry emotional baggage from previous experiences. You may see social withdrawal, hostility, fear, or acting out.

● You'll see a certain amount of grief over the loss of family, especially if the foster child doesn't visit his or her birth family. In cases where the rights of birth parents are severed, the grief reaction will be strong and difficult.

● Foster kids often have problems adjusting to the new environment of the foster home and the subsequent changes involved in moving on to another placement.

What to Say   "I know that all the moving you've done is probably difficult to deal with. How are you doing with it?"

"You've been living with (name of foster parents) for a long time. I'm sure it's hard to leave. How can I help you with it?"

What to Expect   Foster children may avoid developing close relationships because of the possibility of being moved without notice. Therefore, in your initial attempts to get to know the student, you may not get much of a response. However, you will have established what may, in time, become a helping relationship. When a teenager moves out of a foster home, you may observe a variety of responses, ranging from anger and fear to grief over the loss of family. In most cases, foster children will have unresolved issues with their biological parents that they may or may not want to discuss with you.

How to Respond   The key is to let foster children know that you understand their situation and can empathize with them. If they choose to keep to themselves at first, allow them to do so. Keep in mind that adolescents in foster care probably have difficulty trusting people.

How Not to Respond   ● Don't ask for the details of why a student is in foster care. Kids will share this information with you if and when they're ready.

● Don't assume that kids in foster care will be troublemakers. If you do, they'll probably live up to your expectations.

● Don't focus on the negative behaviors kids in foster care may demonstrate. They're often reminded of their behavior problems but may not have heard much about their positive characteristics.

How to Follow Up   Attempt to involve foster kids in your youth group as soon as possible. Foster children want to be just like any other person their age. They may be unsure how to act or what to say at first. The examples set by the rest of the group will help them adjust.

Adolescents who are leaving a foster home may have a difficult time making the transition. You can help them by talking through their plans to move, setting up a time for them to say goodbye to members of the youth group, and encouraging them to look at their new situation positively. If at all possible, keep in contact with foster kids after they leave to reinforce the fact that you care about what happens to them.

Complete the following sentences:

1. The things I like about my foster family are . . .

2. The things I dislike are . . .

3. The worst thing about being in foster care is . . .

4. If I could say anything to my foster parents, I would say . . .

5. The most difficult part of moving is . . .

6. If I could wish for three things, they would be
   a)
   b)
   c)

7. You can help me right now by . . .

This Week

Reflect on Psalm 27 throughout this week. Focus on the images of safety and security.

19. Insights:
Families—Grandparents as Parents

What to Look For — When a family structure changes due to divorce, death, or extreme family problems, grandparents can find themselves to be parents again. Age, fractured dreams of an easy retirement, and resentment toward the circumstances that make them parents can produce a stress overload for everyone involved. This kind of parenting arrangement often causes problems for both the child and the grandparents.

Adolescents in this situation might
- feel grief at the loss of their birth parents.
- be unable to participate in some church activities due to their grandparents' limited retirement income.
- be required to provide care for a grandparent or be more involved in the day-to-day tasks of running a household.

The parenting grandparents might
- feel stressed by the tasks of parenting an active adolescent.
- feel frustrated that age and health prevent them from being as active with their grandchild as they would like.
- struggle to support their second family on a meager retirement income.

What to Say — "Living with grandparents can be a great experience. But it probably has its own set of problems. How is it going for you?"

What to Expect — The question above will allow you to open a conversation with either the student or the grandparents. You may want to talk with either or both about the challenges of their unique family.

Typically the student's response will be more open than the grandparents'. Feeling not just the stress but also a degree of pride in their former and present parenting skills, grandparents may be reluctant to let you or anyone know there is a problem. The exception would be if the grandparent is feeling overwhelmed at the moment.

How to Respond — Listen empathically to the feelings and problems expressed. If you feel the problems have reached a crisis level, you may need to make a referral to a family counselor. Examples of such crises include
- a total breakdown in communication,
- the grandparent feeling overwhelmed to the point of being unable to decide what to do next,
- the adolescent having problems in school or with the law, and
- the possibility of abuse by either the adolescent or the grandparent.

How Not to Respond —
- Avoid making any agreements to deal with one family member on behalf of another. These triangles are never effective.
- Don't delay seeking professional help for the family if you feel help is needed. Older people may feel awkward about seeking outside help, but you'll do them a great service by urging them in that direction.

How to Follow Up — If you've referred the family for help, stay in touch on a regular basis just to see how things are going. You can also be an encourager to these families in a number of other ways:
- Offer an empathic, listening ear to all.
- Provide respite care for the grandparents to give them a temporary break from the parenting role.
- Link the adolescents with other adults in the church who can serve as mentors.

You can empower grandparents by helping them fine-tune their parenting skills through books, videos, workshops, and help with personal problem solving.

Helpsheet 19.

(for teenagers)

1. What do you most enjoy about living with your grandparents?

2. When is living with your grandparents most difficult?

3. What kinds of things do you and your grandparents like to talk about?

4. What is the most important lesson you've learned from your grandparents?

- -

(for grandparents)

1. When do you most enjoy being a parent to your grandchild?

2. What is that makes it a real challenge for you?

3. What's the most important lesson you've learned from your grandchild?

4. Is there anything I can do to help your family at this time?

This Week

Read the story of Abraham, Sarah, and their son, Isaac, in Genesis 21–22. What lessons can you draw from this passage to strengthen your family?

20. Insights:
Families–Harried, Hurried Parents

What to Look For
Family lifestyles have changed dramatically over the past few years. In many two-parent families, both parents work. Single parents are often forced to work more than one job to make ends meet. At times it seems an impossible task for parents to keep up with work, family responsibilities, and kids' school and extracurricular activities. All this scrambling and stress may cause teenagers to experience

- resentment,
- behavior problems,
- depression,
- poor school performance,
- low motivation, and
- conflict with parents.

What to Say
"I've noticed that you don't seem to be getting along well with your mom and dad. They seem to be pretty busy. Do you get to spend much time together?"

What to Expect
Teenagers may give you a very honest answer to this question. However, kids may not have connected their feelings of conflict and frustration to a lack of time with their parents. Parents may be frustrated and defensive when you speak to them.

How to Respond
Explain to parents that the key to getting along with their kids is learning to communicate better. Recognize the demands placed on parents' time, but stress the importance of finding family time. Mention the struggles the child is having, but remember to get the teenager's permission first.

Explain to the teenager that it's normal for kids to want independence, yet it's also necessary to depend on parents for support, encouragement, and direction. Stress the importance of taking advantage of the family time they do have and encourage kids to express their desire to spend more time together. Help teenagers become aware of the important contributions they make to the family.

How Not to Respond
- Don't make excuses for the parents' busy schedules. This will only discourage any change from taking place.
- Don't make excuses for the student's behavior. The student must take responsibility for his or her own behavior. This will reinforce the need to take responsibility for part of the solution to the problem.

How to Follow Up
You can be helpful to this family by mediating between the parents and the teenager. The initial confrontation may be tedious. However, the parents will likely have already felt the strain within the family and may be willing to work at solving the problems. Encourage the family to be creative in developing ways to spend time together. By doing so, you're empowering them to take control and ownership of the positive changes needed in their lives.

1. How could you improve the ways you communicate with each other?

2. What are three strengths of your family?
   a)
   b)
   c)

3. What's the greatest weakness your family struggles with?

4. How much time do you spend together each week?

5. How much time would you like to spend with each other?

   How can you make this possible?

6. Name three things you'd be willing to do this week so you can spend more time together.
   a)
   b)
   c)

7. What goals do you hope to accomplish by spending more time together?

This Week

Read Ephesians 6:1-4. What are the responsibilities of the parent? of the child? Write a paraphrase of this passage that reflects how you can carry out your role. Share your paraphrase with others in your family.

21. Insights:
Families—Single Parent

What to Look For   The assumption that two-parent families are better than single-parent families isn't necessarily correct. This common belief assumes that family configuration—what a family looks like—is more important than family dynamics—how a family functions.

Relationships in a single-parent family may be impacted primarily by two factors. The first is the resolution of the issues contributing to the breakup of the parents' marriage. The second factor is the challenge to care for and support the family. Kids from single-parent families are often impacted by

● stress, due to the financial struggles of a single-income household;

● loneliness, due to having more time alone while Mom or Dad works long hours or more than one job; and

● social isolation, often due to over-exposure to television, the entertainment choice of financially limited households.

What to Say   "How's it going for you now that it's just you and your mom (or dad) living together?"

What to Expect   Assuming you have a good relationship with the student, you can expect to receive a fairly open and straightforward response. If the student doesn't seem open, don't press it. By simply asking, you have communicated a message of caring and have invited the student to engage in future conversation.

How to Respond   If the student responds openly to you, don't hesitate to explore any concerns you have. Use Helpsheet 21 to determine how the student is handling the changes that have occurred within the family. Listen particularly for responses that suggest difficulty with stress, loneliness, or social isolation.

How Not to Respond   Avoid buying into any of these hurtful, damaging myths about single-parent families:

● Single parents are more sexually promiscuous than other single adults.

● Single parents are always women.

● Fathers abandon their children financially, physically, and emotionally after a divorce in which the mother gets custody or primary physical care of the child.

● Kids from single-parent families are more troubled and unhappy than kids from intact, two-parent families.

Beware of these and any other myths about single-parent families. What you believe will influence your response to the adolescents involved.

How to Follow Up   Empower and encourage kids from single-parent homes by making yourself available and letting these kids tell you what they need and how you can help them. If students need to learn new skills for their new family situations, offer to teach them. For example, an adolescent may be more familiar with one parent's neighborhood than the other's. The student may need to learn how to meet people and make new friends in the less familiar neighborhood.

Be aware of how family finances and visitation schedules impact students' involvement in your church and group. Help kids find ways to stay connected. Cheer their attempts to adjust to their new family situations. Encourage their efforts to build solid relationships and successful families.

Helpsheet 21.

Complete the following sentences:

1. The changes I like in my family are...

2. The changes that are most uncomfortable for me are...

3. I'm most afraid of any change that will result in...

4. One thing that will not change between Mom and me is...

5. One thing that will not change between Dad and me is...

6. The change I could use the most help with now is...

This Week

Read Psalm 136. What does it mean for me and my family that "God's love continues forever"?

Permission to photocopy this helpsheet granted for local church use.
Copyright © Tom Klaus and Lamar Roth. Published in *Counseling Helpsheets* by Group Publishing, Inc., Box 481, Loveland, CO 80539.

22. Insights: Friendships—Making Friends

What to Look For — Making friends is becoming a lost art in our society. Perhaps this trend is a result of the rootlessness of American families and the emphasis on individual entertainment through television and video games. Whatever the reasons, kids who are having a hard time making friends are pretty easy to spot. We see them
- off by themselves at group functions;
- making awkward, even inappropriate, attempts to interact with people through teasing, loud or rude comments, attempting to dominate conversations, or name-dropping;
- trying to "buy" friends with gifts;
- being made fun of; and
- trying to acquire friends by bullying or threats.

What to Say — "I've noticed that you're trying hard to make friends, but you aren't having too much luck. I've got some ideas that could help. Are you interested?"

What to Expect — Rarely will a person turn down an opportunity to learn how to make friends. Kids who are really eager to gain new friends may feel embarrassed to know that anyone else has seen their failure. However, they will usually welcome your assistance.

How to Respond — If your offer is turned down, just let it go. By extending the invitation, you've indicated that you're aware of a problem. And you've identified yourself as a person who is willing to help.

If your offer is received, use Helpsheet 22 as a guide to teaching basic friend-making skills.

How Not to Respond — Don't make light of kids' struggle to make friends. Teaching kids how to make friends is a lot like teaching them about personal hygiene. It requires sensitivity to their feelings. Actually, you may need to teach about sensitive issues like personal hygiene if you sense it is a reason people are avoiding their attempts to make friends.

How to Follow Up — Plan to meet individually with the student for a few weeks to monitor his or her progress and practice skills needed in making friends. You will encourage kids through regular appointments and celebrating successes. Empowerment through modeling, instruction, and practice are important, too. Let your friendship with these students be a model for friendship they can create with others. Use the time together to evaluate progress and teach new skills through role-playing.

1. Those who are successful in making new friends believe they can be good friends themselves. What is it about you that makes you a "good friend"?

2. It's not always easy to accept the idea that there might be some things about us that make it hard for others to become our friends. What might make it hard for someone to become your friend?

3. We all have traits we can't change—things that people just have to accept. But we also have traits we can change so it's easier for others to accept us. Of the things you just mentioned in your answer to question 2, which can't be changed? Which can?

4. What personal traits do you want to start changing today? Prioritize the changes you'd like to see in yourself.

5. For each trait you'd like to change, brainstorm a plan for change using this pattern.
a) Identify your goal. What personal trait do you want to change?

b) What do you need to do or learn to meet this goal? Be as specific as possible.

c) How will you do it or learn it?

d) How will you know when you've met the goal?

6. When shall we meet again to celebrate the changes you're making and work on new friendship skills?

This Week

One of the best friendships recorded in the Bible was the friendship between David and Jonathan. Read about them in the book of 1 Samuel 18–20. Look for the things that made theirs a good friendship. Then think of ways you can make those same qualities a part of your friendships.

23. Insights:
Friendships—Keeping Friends

What to Look For Making new friends can be the easiest part of friendship. Maintaining friendships over a long period can be a challenge. You can identify kids who have a hard time keeping friends when you see any or all of these patterns:

● "Closed door" friendships—It's a normal part of adolescence to have numerous friendships, many of which are on again, off again. These "open door" friendships are able to accommodate the fickle whims of adolescence. As kids mature, friendships tend to become more stable. When kids aren't able to easily re-enter relationships, we say they've "closed the door" on the friendship.

● Lowered standards for friendships— When kids can't keep the friends they want, they may change their standards for friendship and begin to accept behaviors and qualities which had previously been unacceptable. This happens when kids begin to hang out with groups that represent values and behaviors which are different from their own.

● Social withdrawal—When kids have trouble keeping good friends, they are at risk of becoming socially withdrawn, depressed, or even involved in destructive relationships.

What to Say "I've noticed recently that you seem to be having a tough time keeping friends. I'm wondering if I could help with some ideas for making your friendships work. Are you interested?"

What to Expect Defensiveness is one possible response. None of us likes to be reminded that we're failing in our friendships. If a students turns you down, it might be a matter of pride. Be content with the knowledge that you've expressed your concern and extended your offer of help. Kids will remember that.

Because it hurts to lose friends, expect your sincere, caring offer to be well-received.

How to Respond Allow the student to talk about how it feels to lose friends. Helpsheet 23 will guide you in drawing out those feelings and helping the student discover the keys to successful long-term relationships.

How Not to Respond Avoid offering a critique of the student's friendship style. Well-meaning critiques have a way of sounding like harsh criticism when you're addressing something as personal as this.

How to Follow Up Plan to meet individually with the student for a few weeks to monitor his or her progress. Offer encouragement by celebrating his or her successes. Empowerment through modeling, instruction, and practice are important, too. Use the time together to evaluate progress and teach new skills through role-playing and discussion. Let your friendship with the student be a model for friendships he or she can enjoy with others.

1. In order to keep a friendship strong and healthy, both people must be willing to work at it. Even if you really want a friendship to last, the other person can choose to end it. Think of a friendship that ended recently. Did it end because the other person wanted it to end? because you wanted it to end? Or did it just happen? Explain.

2. List several characteristics you want in a good friend.

3. If you expect these things from a good friend, that friend probably expects the same things from you. Think again about the list you just created. Explain how others might see these qualities in you. For instance, if you listed "commitment," you might say, "I'd be there to talk when things were tough."

4. What can you change in the way you relate to your friends to make sure those friendships will last?

5. Name two people you'd like to build stronger friendships with starting this week.

This Week

Read the story of the friendship between Barnabas and Paul in Acts 9:1-30; 11:19-26; 12:25–13:5; 13:42–15:12; 15:36-41. What do you think Paul and Barnabas could have done to save their friendship?

24. Insights:
Friendships—Losing or Changing Friends

What to Look For   You'll know when friendships among the kids in your group end. If you don't notice it in casual conversation and contact with them, you'll hear about it from others. It's important to approach a student who has lost a friend or group of friends if you see any of these problems:
- moodiness,
- social withdrawal or isolation,
- a negative attitude, or
- a failure to attend group functions.

What to Say   "I've noticed that you and _____ don't seem to be spending much time together. Do you want to talk about it?"

What to Expect   Expect a positive response. If the student is having a tough time, the opportunity to talk about the loss will be a welcome invitation.

If the student declines, feel comfortable with the fact that you've opened the door for future conversations.

How to Respond   Listen empathically as the student explains his or her feeling of loss. Then use Helpsheet 24 to help the student understand the steps to recovery.

How Not to Respond
- Don't minimize the loss with comments such as "You'll get over it."

- Avoid trying to find new friends for the student by suggesting names of people he or she could befriend.

How to Follow Up   Your primary role is to be an encourager. Be in informal, regular contact with students who are dealing with the loss of friends. Kids will feel cared for and encouraged by your interest in their well-being.

It's important to remember that kids who have lost good friends are grieving. Grief of that nature can't be processed quickly or easily, especially if the friendships were close and had lasted for years. Be patient. People deal with loss and pain in their own way. You may not understand why a student feels so hurt about losing a friendship you thought was insignificant, but you must appreciate the loss he or she feels.

1. Tell me something about your friendship with _____. How did you get to be friends? How did your friendship grow?

2. What made your friendship special?

3. What happened to change your friendship? When did you notice this change? What do you think could have been done to avoid ending the friendship?

4. Ten years from now, what's the first thing you'll remember when you think of this friendship?

5. What can I do to help you through this tough time?

This Week

Read Psalm 27:10. How does it feel to know that God is a friend who will never forsake you?

25. Insights: Peer Pressure

What to Look For   Positive peer pressure never concerns us. It's when we see kids being affected by negative peer groups that we worry. Because of the unique relationship a youth worker has with kids, you'll probably see the influence of negative peer groups in a student's life before the parents or other adults do.

It's common for adolescents to change peer groups as a means of trying new ideas and behaviors. Withdrawal from regular activity in one group to become more involved in another is normal. It's when a student's involvement in a new group seems to require exclusion of all other contact that you need to be concerned.

Consider intervening if you see these problems developing:

- dramatic mood changes, possibly related to drug or alcohol abuse;
- destructive behaviors that are potentially harmful to the student and others;
- isolation from individuals and groups that had previously been important to the student; and
- reports of gang pressure or activity.

What to Say   "You seem to be making changes in your friendships. While it's great to make new friends, I'm concerned about some changes I've seen in you. Would you like to know what I'm seeing?"

What to Expect   If the student is still on the fringes of a new peer group, you are likely to win a hearing with your invitation. If the student is already deeply involved, you are more likely to receive a "thanks, but no thanks" response.

How to Respond   If you receive the green light to share your observations, do so in a nonjudgmental but concerned way. Use the questions on Helpsheet 25 to discover what has motivated the student to make changes in his or her circle of friends.

When students indicate an unwillingness to talk, simply affirm your continuing love and concern and invite them to come to you any time in the future. Then move to a safer subject and just talk for a while. By doing this, you'll strengthen your relationship for a time when you might need to attempt to intervene again.

How Not to Respond   It's important not to attack members of the student's new peer group. Doing so would be counterproductive and would only strengthen the bond the student already feels with the group.

Don't preach to kids. Avoid the temptation to use this opportunity to get kids to make a stronger commitment to your youth program.

How to Follow Up   Stay in touch, even if the student chooses not to speak with you. Your frequent, caring contact will be an encouragement. The student will know you're a safe person to approach if trouble comes.

If the student is open to hearing your concerns and expresses a desire for help, play an empowering role by teaching him or her how to make and keep new friends (see Helpsheets 22 and 23).

Any time you see a student participating in destructive behavior, contact his or her parents. Encourage the parents to notify the proper authorities and seek professional counseling.

1. What is it about your new friends that makes you enjoy their company?

2. What is there about your new friends that sometimes bothers you?

3. What was there about your old group that turned you off?

4. Is there anything you miss about your old friends?

5. How can you keep and enjoy your old friends as well as your new ones?

6. How can I help you keep friendships in both groups?

This Week

The 12 disciples were a special group of friends to Jesus. Jesus carefully taught them about the kingdom of God. Read Matthew 5–7. These are some of the most important lessons and truths Jesus taught his friends. Would you be comfortable sharing these truths with your friends?

26. Insights: Physical Abuse

What to Look For Teenagers who have been physically abused or are currently being abused act out in a variety of ways. If you suspect someone is being abused, report it immediately. See Part Three for information on reporting abuse. Here we'll focus on dealing with the student after the reports and appropriate interventions have taken place. Any of these problem behaviors may remain well after the abuse has ceased:

- an avoidance of adults,
- excessive withdrawal,
- aggressiveness,
- poor academic performance,
- depression,
- hopelessness,
- generalized anger,
- running away from home,
- an inability to develop and sustain relationships,
- substance abuse and other illegal behavior, and
- suicidal thoughts and behavior.

What to Say "I imagine things are pretty confusing for you right now. When someone has been hurt and abused the way you have, they're not always sure how to deal with it. How are you handling it?"

What to Expect You need to expect any of several possible responses. The student might give no response at all or simply dismiss you with a statement that everything is OK. You are an adult and the teenager may not be ready to trust adults yet. Kids who have been abused have a need to take care of themselves, and they feel that they can do a better job of it than the adults in their lives.

Other kids may need to tell you about their abuse over and over again. This repetition fulfills their need to somehow make sense of the abuse. They may even speak favorably of the abuser. If the abuser was a parent, the student may continue to demonstrate love and a strong emotional attachment to the abuser.

How to Respond If kids choose to remain silent, respect that choice, but let them know you'd be glad to talk with them in the future. If kids are willing to talk, use the listening skills described in Part One. Be patient when kids begin to share how they're feeling and tell what they've experienced.

When outside authorities and professionals get involved in abuse investigations, kids often feel abandoned. Let them know that the abuse they suffered is inexcusable and that you'll stand by them no matter what.

How Not to Respond
- Don't ask about the details of the abuse.
- Be careful not to use questions or statements that may insinuate that the adolescent is responsible for being abused. Victims of abuse tend to blame themselves. Don't say anything that could reinforce that belief.
- Don't pressure kids to talk about the abuse. Since these kids have been controlled and manipulated, they need to take control of what they say about the abuse, when they say it, and who they trust with the information.
- Don't make excuses for the abuser. Making excuses would cause the student to experience more guilt and eventually lose trust in you.

How to Follow Up The effects of physical abuse in the family and the individual are deep and complex. The most positive possible outcome is for the physical and emotional pain to be addressed, allowing the family to come back together and function in a healthy way. This may happen to varying degrees or not at all.

You'll probably need to provide long-term support. And there may be setbacks. Eventually, the adolescent will have to take responsibility for his or her own actions and responses. Your role may be to gently confront kids who have been abused and encourage them to own their feelings and behaviors.

Unfortunately, abuse in families often recurs. Be aware of this possibility and be ready to report all incidents of abuse to the authorities. While this is a difficult thing to do, the safety of the adolescent and others in his or her family is the top priority. Until the abuse stops, there cannot be healing for the victims or the family.

Helpsheet 26.

Complete the following sentences:

1. The thing that I am most afraid of is . . .

2. A father should . . .

3. A mother should . . .

4. I wish my family would . . .

5. When I think of when I was abused by _____, I feel like I could . . .

6. The most important thing that I learned about myself through the abuse that I suffered is . . .

7. If I could change three things in my life, I would change
   a)
   b)
   c)

This Week

Read Psalm 31. Which of the feelings expressed in the psalm can you identify with? Which parts of the psalm give you hope for healing and a better future?

27. Insights: Romantic Attraction

What to Look For
The rush of a new romance is incredible for people of any age, but especially for adolescents. Numerous physical and emotional changes beginning at puberty conspire to make being in love one of the most powerful experiences students will have during their journey into adulthood.

Adolescents fall in and out of love very quickly and intensely. When they're falling in love, the world couldn't be a better place. But when they're falling out of love, they may need you to help them hold their world together. Oddly enough, the symptoms of falling in love are very similar to the symptoms of falling out of love. You may see

● an obsession with the other person demonstrated by an inability to focus or concentrate and incessant talking about the person;

● mood swings that match the ups and downs of the relationship; and

● social isolation, in order either to spend every free minute with the other person or to heal from the ending of the romance.

What to Say
"How is it going with _____?"

What to Expect
If you have a solid, trusting relationship with the student, you may expect him or her to give you a complete update.

How to Respond
Listen to the student talk about the relationship; ask questions about the new love. Be alert for details that tell you whether the couple is developing a healthy or unhealthy relationship. Healthy relationships will be characterized by mutual respect, trust, and honesty. If the relationship is developing along these lines, great!

How Not to Respond
● Don't underestimate the intensity of the emotions of a teenager in love. Respect those feelings even if they don't seem fully mature.

● Never overlook a teenager's response to a breakup. Be watchful and stay in touch. It's not uncommon for teens to become suicidal when they've lost at love. Any time you suspect a student's breakup is causing him or her to think thoughts of self-destruction or harm to another person, be prepared to make a referral to the proper authorities.

How to Follow Up
Your interest (not teasing!) will be encouraging to a student as his or her relationship with a special person develops. If you're present when things are going well, the student is likely to involve you when things begin to go badly.

Recognize that teenagers in love tend to have a low tolerance for unsolicited counsel from adults. If your counsel is forced, it won't be received. Explain that you have some concerns about the relationship and ask if the student would like to hear them. If he or she gives permission, proceed with caution, understanding that if you become "preachy" you risk being shut out.

If your concerns are received, you can offer to help the student work on the relationship. Helpsheet 27 will guide you in identifying values that are important in making romantic and sexual choices.

You might have the student read and discuss *The Next Time I Fall in Love* by Chap Clark (Zondervan). This process will help the student put the relationship in perspective and gain valuable information for future relationships.

1. On a scale of 1 (never any romance) to 10 (always very romantic), identify how romantic each period of a relationship should be.

	Never Any Romance								Always Very Romantic	
First Meeting	1	2	3	4	5	6	7	8	9	10
First Date	1	2	3	4	5	6	7	8	9	10
Going Steady	1	2	3	4	5	6	7	8	9	10
Engagement	1	2	3	4	5	6	7	8	9	10
Marriage	1	2	3	4	5	6	7	8	9	10
Fifth Anniversary	1	2	3	4	5	6	7	8	9	10
10th Anniversary	1	2	3	4	5	6	7	8	9	10

2. At what point do you think people first realize they're in love? Circle one.

first meeting   first date   going steady   engagement   marriage

3. At what point do you think commitment becomes important to most people? Circle one.

first meeting   first date   going steady   engagement   marriage

4. At what point do you think it's OK to become sexually active with your partner? Circle one.

first meeting   first date   going steady   engagement   marriage

5. How far do you think most love relationships that begin at your age will go? Circle one.

first meeting   first date   going steady   engagement   marriage

This Week

Read I Corinthians 13 and compare your goals for romance with this model of a loving relationship.

28. Insights: School

What to Look For   Unless a student comes to you with a complaint about school, you're most likely to learn of school problems through parents. Some of the problems you may hear about are

- cutting class,
- truancy,
- low grades,
- discipline problems,
- fighting with other students, and
- unfair treatment from a teacher.

What to Say   "It sounds like school's been kind of rough lately. What do you think is going on?"

What to Expect   When a student comes to you with a complaint about school, expect a gush of information about the problem. The same is generally true when you approach a student with information you received from the parent.

Another possible response is denial that a problem even exists—and this could be true. Some parents are more invested in their child's schooling than the child is. Therefore, what parents perceive to be a problem may not seem like a problem to the child.

How to Respond   Students who complain of a problem with a teacher may need your help in brainstorming possible solutions.

If you've approached a student about reported school problems, remember two things:

1. School is a common rebellion ground for normal adolescents.

2. Poor school performance can be a symptom of other, more serious problems such as family stress, drug or alcohol abuse, learning disabilities, early gang involvement, or attention deficit (hyperactivity) disorder.

Since you're not qualified to clearly determine which of these is happening, you need to make a referral to someone who can. Most schools have resources and programs to assess kids' school performance and determine what underlying factors are contributing to the problem.

How Not to Respond   Don't speak to a student on behalf of a parent. Avoid stepping into a parenting role. It's best to be a consultant to the parents, helping them speak directly to the child about their concerns.

How to Follow Up   Empowerment, encouragement, and referral are useful to kids who are struggling at school. When students complain of difficulty with teachers, you can help by teaching them assertiveness and encouraging them to communicate clearly with the teachers about the problems.

When students come to you with problems documented by the school, encourage them (and their parents) to take advantage of services at the school or in the community that can address the problems. During the time kids are receiving these services, stay in touch and affirm their efforts to resolve the problems.

1. When is school most enjoyable for you?

2. When is it least enjoyable?

3. How are you feeling about school right now?

It's the pits.				It's OK.					It's great!
1	2	3	4	5	6	7	8	9	10

4. How does your experience at school make you feel about yourself right now?

I'm lousy.				I'm OK.					I'm great!
1	2	3	4	5	6	7	8	9	10

5. What do you think needs to happen to make school a better place for you?

6. What can you do to make this happen?

7. How will you do it?

This Week

Read Proverbs 4. How important is it to you to gain wisdom? What part does school play in gaining wisdom? How does this passage challenge you to make the most of your school experience?

29. Insights: Sexual Abuse

What to Look For
Teenagers who have been sexually abused or are currently being abused act out in a variety of ways. If you suspect abuse, report it immediately to the proper authorities. You'll find instructions for referral in Part Three. Here, we'll help you deal with the adolescent after the abuse has been reported and appropriate interventions have taken place. Any of these problem behaviors may continue well after the abuse has been stopped:

● extreme fear for no apparent reason,
● intense anger,
● an inability to trust others,
● depression,
● a decline in school performance,
● eating disorders,
● running away from home,
● problems sleeping, and
● inappropriate sexual behavior and promiscuity.

What to Say
"I know you've been going through a lot lately, and I've been thinking of you. Tell me, how have you been handling it?"

What to Expect
People who have been sexually abused usually feel confused, guilty, and angry. They may tell you they're OK either because they don't trust you, they're not sure how to put their feelings into words, they're confused, or they're ashamed of what happened.

Parents of a sexually abused child respond the same way. They may deny that any problems exist in the hope that the problems will solve themselves or go away. Their denial is often so strong that it takes considerable time before they're able to face the problems at all.

Sometimes the adolescent is unwilling to talk about the abuse with someone who is the same sex as the abuser. In this case, it's best to have the student work with someone who has expertise in this area and is not the same sex as the abuser.

How to Respond
If students choose not to share with you, let them know that you'd be willing to listen later on if and when they feel more comfortable. Be aware that the adolescent is weighing the risk of sharing this information with you and may not be willing to take such a risk yet. If a student does share with you, be slow to make recommendations and quick to offer consolation and understanding. If the student isn't in therapy with a professional, suggest it.

How Not to Respond
● Don't expect to help a student through the effects of sexual abuse on your own.
● Never suggest that the student encouraged the abuse.
● Don't ask for details. The adolescent has probably had to tell the story too many times already, and the information is too private for you to examine. If a student brings up details of the abuse, gently explain that you have no need to know them. Then move the discussion to feeling levels and behavior issues.
● Don't make excuses for the abuser.
● Don't place yourself in a vulnerable position. Be careful of physical contact or being alone with the student. Some teenagers' perceptions of touch are distorted.

How to Follow Up
If the adolescent is seeing a qualified therapist, it's likely the family is also involved. The support of the family is extremely important to the teenager at this time. Because the teenager and the family often feel alone and isolated, your support and encouragement are greatly needed. Remember that recovery and healing may take a long time. Sustain your ministry to them as long as they need it.

Complete the following sentences:

1. The thing I'm most afraid of is . . .

2. If only I could . . .

3. The most important thing I've learned about myself is . . .

4. If I could change three things in my life I would change
a)
b)
c)

5. What I need most in my life is . . .

6. When I look at myself in the mirror I see . . .

7. My parents . . .

This Week

Read Psalm 31. How are King David's cries like feelings you've experienced? What hope and encouragement can you find in this psalm?

30. Insights: Sexual Risk Taking

What to Look For   Sexual experimentation is often a part of adolescence. Youth workers commonly expend considerable energy trying to prevent couples from pairing off at retreats and other activities. We use the term "sexual risk taking" because no generation has been at greater risk of contracting sexually transmitted diseases, not to mention the spiritual and emotional risks involved in premarital sex.

We take this reality-based approach to sexuality issues: While we encourage kids to save sex for marriage, we recognize that many don't wait. As a result, in addition to encouraging abstinence, we feel it's important to talk to kids who have become sexually active about options for protected sex. Early intervention is possible through group prevention programs or talking with students when you see these warning signs:

- raging hormones,
- pairing off, and
- couples spending a lot of time alone.

What to Say   "Adolescence can be a crazy time when it comes to sex. It can be so easy to give in to pressure or temptations that put you at risk of disease or pregnancy and strain your relationship with God. How are you handling the pressure?"

What to Expect   You'll probably open this conversation with an adolescent you suspect is becoming sexually active. The student may fidget a bit and seem uncomfortable with your question. Keep in mind that sex is a personal subject, so this discomfort is normal—it doesn't necessarily mean that the student is already having sexual intercourse. Don't be surprised if the student gives you a fast answer to deflect additional questions.

How to Respond   Be calm, patient, and sensitive to the student's feelings of awkwardness. If the student seems too uncomfortable, you may want to back off unless there is a crisis that requires you to pursue the conversation. If the student initiates the conversation, realize that he or she is feeling some concern or guilt. Let grace be the rule you follow. Listen empathically, then use Helpsheet 30 to guide your conversation.

How Not to Respond   • Don't be voyeuristic, digging for details you don't need to know.

• Avoid condemning a student who's become sexually active. Condemnation destroys a relationship, and this is the time when the student needs you more than ever. Not condemning doesn't mean you can't share your own values about premature sexual activity. It simply means you should be careful and gracious with the timing and tone of what you say.

How to Follow Up   Few parents feel comfortable talking with their kids about sexuality issues. As a result, the task of sex education has fallen largely on schools and the church. You may be one of the primary sources of information on sexuality for the students in your ministry.

You can encourage kids by being a friendly adult presence in the midst of one of the most confusing times in adolescence.

Be available and willing to talk to students about sex and sexuality. Establish a relationship of trust and comfort that will support these kinds of conversations.

Empower kids to reduce the spiritual, emotional, and physical risks of sexual activity by teaching about abstinence and sexuality issues. While sex education in the church may be difficult to initiate, it's an essential part of ministering to the whole person.

Helpsheet 30.

(for teenagers who are practicing abstinence)

1. Tell me what has helped you say no.

2. What's the toughest part about waiting to have sex with someone?

3. How do you handle the pressure you get from
   a) friends who encourage you to have sex?
   b) your dating partner?
   c) your own body?

4. In view of 1 Corinthians 6:18-20, how will you know when you're ready for a sexual relationship?

5. What can I do to help you wait until the time you are ready?

This Week

First Corinthians 3:16 and 6:18-20 teach us that our bodies are the dwelling place of God through the Holy Spirit. How does keeping yourself pure affect the way you feel about your body? How does it affect your relationship with God?

(for teenagers who are sexually active)

1. How do you know a sexual relationship is right for you at this time?

2. How does the choice to be sexually active fit with what you believe about yourself, about God, and about your relationship with your partner?

3. Are you aware of the risks of being sexually active with someone?

4. What steps are you taking to protect yourself from disease and pregnancy?

5. What can I do to help you reduce the risks of a sexual relationship?

This Week

First Corinthians 3:16 and 6:18-20 teach us that our bodies are the dwelling place of God through the Holy Spirit. How does sexual activity affect the way you feel about your body? How does it affect your relationship with God?

31. Insights: Spiritual and Moral Development

What to Look For
During adolescence, kids form, test, and re-form ideas which will eventually become the foundation of their spirituality and morality. This process allows them to "own" their faith. Parents and youth workers often misunderstand this testing and challenging process, interpreting it as rebellion. We don't agree. It's been our experience that when students aren't given the opportunity to challenge and test their beliefs in a secure, stable environment, more serious rebellion is likely to occur later on.

Students who are developing their spiritual and moral identities frequently feel intense internal anxiety. This anxiety stems from their struggle to discover what's right and to verify by their own experience what they've been taught. As a youth worker, it's important to accept this process as a healthy sign of growth. You should become concerned, however, if you see students

● struggle with depression for two weeks or longer as a result of making behavioral choices which are in conflict with their beliefs,

● fail to evaluate and adjust behaviors or re-form beliefs and values that are in conflict, or

● unable to process intense feelings of guilt.

What to Say
"I've noticed that you've seemed really down the last few days. There seems to be a lot weighing on you. Would you like to talk?"

What to Expect
Students who are experiencing the anxiety of spiritual formation will usually be eager to talk. However, don't be surprised if they have a hard time identifying the problem and giving it a name. It may come across as a "generalized anxiety."

How to Respond
● Listen. Then offer encouragement and grace.

● Consider sharing with students the spiritual journals of great Christians such as Martin Luther, C.S. Lewis, or St. Francis of Assisi. These writers describe the intense agony they experienced as they confronted the claims of Christianity and discovered their own spiritual and moral selves. Use Helpsheet 31 to guide your efforts to encourage and empower students on this part of their spiritual pilgrimage.

● If a student appears to be struggling with depression, be prepared to refer him or her to a mental-health professional.

How Not to Respond
● Avoid guilt trips. The experience of spiritual formation often carries with it intense feelings of guilt or conviction. Be helpful and nonjudgmental as you allow students to express their uncertainties.

● Don't rush the process. Let students work through faith issues at their own pace. If they can't complete the work now, they may go through the whole painful process again.

How to Follow Up
Invite the student to meet with you any time he or she needs to talk. In the meantime, stay in frequent, informal contact. Encourage the student with your interest and willingness to listen. Empower the student by sharing your own spiritual struggles and offering gentle counsel when the student requests it. Be careful not to offer counsel too quickly—it's best to let the student invite you into the process. But when the invitation comes, be prepared to offer an honest look at your own process of spiritual growth.

1. You seem to be in a battle with yourself. What can you tell me about the two sides?

2. Circle the words that describe how you feel right now.

angry	frustrated	depressed	excited	bothered	anxious
guilty	happy	irritated	worried	blue	content

other feelings: _____

3. Which of those feelings are most intense?

4. When did you first notice the feelings? What do you think brought them on?

5. How do these feelings relate to your faith?

6. How can I support your efforts to resolve these feelings?

This Week

Read the stories of these Bible characters who struggled with their faith. What can you learn about your own spiritual struggle by reading about theirs?
- Moses—Exodus 3:1–4:17
- Ruth—the book of Ruth
- Jonah—the book of Jonah
- a father—Mark 9:17-27

32. Insights:
Substance Abuse and Dependence

What to Look For Substance abuse is a continuing problem among teenagers. Kids may experiment with alcohol or drugs in order to satisfy their curiosity, in response to pressure from peers, or to mimic the behavior of adults. The adolescent who continues to abuse alcohol or drugs can develop a physical and/or psychological dependence. This may happen quickly or over a long period of time, depending on the type of substance used and the emotional issues the adolescent is facing. Symptoms of dependence are

- dramatic changes in personality;
- a decline in school performance;
- a lack of interest in activities that were once important;
- legal problems;
- an inability to fulfill obligations at home, school, or work;
- trying unsuccessfully to quit;
- spending time and energy obtaining the substance;
- increased usage in order to obtain the same effect; and
- taking other substances to relieve withdrawal symptoms.

We do not want to represent ourselves as experts in the area of substance abuse and dependence. Our practice is to refer students to programs and persons who specialize in this area. You'll find information on making such a referral in Part Three.

What to Say "I know you've been drinking quite a bit, and it appears to be causing you some real problems. How do you see it?"

What to Expect Denial. In most cases, kids we have talked to won't admit that their usage is a problem. They'll try to turn the tables and say, "I don't have a problem—it's the people who are complaining about it who have a problem." Kids frequently minimize how much or how often they use drugs or alcohol. For instance, a student who claims to have had only one drink may actually have consumed one very large or potent drink, one bottle, or one six- or twelve-pack of beer.

How to Respond Confronting out of genuine concern is the most effective way to reach students who are abusing substances. Assume that kids will deny or minimize their addiction. When you ask if they have a problem, they'll deny it. Let them know that you believe they have a problem and be specific about what you observe in their behavior or personality that leads you to this conclusion.

How Not to Respond
- Don't allow their attempts at minimizing and denial to go unchallenged.
- Don't indicate that you condone the behavior.
- Don't attempt to handle this problem on your own.

How to Follow Up It's important to refer the student and parents to a qualified alcohol and drug counselor. Check in with them from time to time to see how the counseling is going. The counselor may recommend that the student join a support group such as Alcoholics Anonymous or Narcotics Anonymous. These groups provide a good support system with confrontation and modeling. Give the family your ongoing support and encouragement throughout the counseling process.

Helpsheet 32.

1. How often are you drinking or using (substance)?

2. What problems has your use of (substance) caused?

3. When did you begin using (substance)?

4. Who do you use (substance) with?

5. When you drink or use (substance), how does it make you feel? Do you like the way it makes you feel?

6. Have you tried to stop drinking or using (substance)? Have you been successful?

7. When you are not using (substance), how do you feel about yourself?

8. What would you like to change about your life?

This Week

Read 1 Corinthians 6:12, 19-20. What does it mean to be "mastered" by something? What choices does God give us? Thinking back over the last few months, what choices would you change?

33. Insights: Suicide

What to Look For
Working with a suicidal adolescent can be difficult and tedious. It's important to get a suicidal teenager involved in therapy with a qualified professional. In Part Three you'll find further information on referral. Your role is to support the student and to encourage him or her to work through troubling issues. The following indicators will alert you that an adolescent may be suicidal:

- depression,
- low self-worth,
- a change in personality,
- difficulty concentrating,
- the loss of someone important,
- problems at home and school,
- loss of motivation and interest, and
- embarrassment about previous suicidal actions.

What to Say
"I'm concerned about you after the way you talked about killing yourself. How are you feeling about yourself today?"

What to Expect
A student may be embarrassed about the incident and tell you that everything is OK now. Or, the student may be willing to tell you what led him or her to thoughts of suicide. It's likely that the circumstances are still unresolved and that the student may continue to be bothered by suicidal thoughts.

How to Respond
Help the student get the issues out in the open. A direct approach is best. Even if the student is in therapy, your support is still important. Suicidal teenagers usually feel that they lack the skills and support necessary to deal with their problems.

How Not to Respond
- Don't avoid talking directly about the suicidal thoughts or attempt—bring the subject out into the open.
- Don't suggest that suicidal teens are wrong to feel the way they do. The fact is, they do feel hopeless and need help to move beyond those feelings.
- Don't attempt to make them feel guilty by labeling their behavior as sinful or pointing out to them how suicide hurts those who love them.
- Don't accept statements such as "I'm OK now." Kids may say that to avoid dealing with their real problems.

How to Follow Up
We recommend that you keep in regular contact with adolescents who express thoughts of suicide. Check in regularly to see how they're doing. If they are in therapy with a mental-health professional, they may be working on some very difficult and sensitive issues. Support this process and allow them to use you as a sounding board. Do all you can to keep them involved with your youth group. That will reinforce a sense of belonging and self-worth.

We also recommend that you have regular contact with the parents. They will experience periods of confusion, fear, and anger as well. If the parents aren't in the therapy process with the child, encourage them to get involved.

Help kids work out a safety plan they can put into effect when they're feeling suicidal. For example, they could call you or their therapists. They could call a local crisis line. (See the information on page 100 of Part Three about community-resource directories.) They could also confide in their parents or close friends who know what steps to take to keep them safe. We suggest that you draw up a contract together that outlines the safety plan in detail. Then both of you can sign and date the contract. This process reinforces a sense of responsibility, accountability, and support.

Complete the following sentences:

1. When I think about suicide, I feel . . .

2. What bothers me the most right now is . . .

3. My level of depression or sadness right now is . . .

none				somewhat depressed				very depressed	
1	2	3	4	5	6	7	8	9	10

4. If I could change three things in my life I would change
a)
b)
c)

5. When I feel depressed and suicidal you can help me by . . .

6. When I look at myself in the mirror I see . . .

7. What I would like to see is . . .

This Week

Read Psalm 42. How are the feelings David expresses like your feelings? Where does David find a source of hope? Where can you find sources of hope? Write down three things you can thank God for.

34. Insights: Teenage Dad

What to Look For

Teenage fathers are not as obvious as teenage moms. Unless he steps forward or is pointed out by the pregnant girl, you may never know the father of the baby about to be born to that sophomore girl in your youth group. Unless a teenage father steps forward willingly, most efforts at counseling will be in vain. Those who make contact under pressure from the mother and her family seldom cooperate.

What to Say

"This must be quite a surprise for you. What can I do to help?"

What to Expect

A teenage father-to-be who seeks your help is going to be quite willing to accept it. He may not, however, be willing to fully accept the responsibility of his position. As he learns more about the decisions that need to be made— the necessity of establishing paternity if he wants to be involved with his child and responsibilities of child support if he and the mom don't marry—you may see him trying to quickly back away.

How to Respond

- First, ask about the teenage father's health. If he has not been tested for sexually transmitted diseases or HIV, strongly encourage him to be tested. If he's a carrier, the baby could be infected. The mother's doctor needs this information as soon as possible.
- Clarify what he plans to do about his relationship with the mother and the baby, if she decides to keep it.
- Be prepared to refer the young father and his family for counseling and medical and support services such as a young-dads group.
- Explain to the young father that if he wishes to be assured of access to his child after its birth, he may need to establish legal paternity. Be prepared with a referral to an attorney who practices family or domestic law.

How Not to Respond

- Even though you may have taught about the physical and spiritual consequences of premarital sex, this is not the time to say, "I told you so." Choose grace as your response.
- None of the choices facing a teenage dad is easy. Don't push him or his family into the choice you prefer. Speak of grace, forgiveness, and God's provision. But remember that the teenager is responsible to God for his own actions. You can't take responsibility for him. The young man has to make his own decision and live with the consequences.

How to Follow Up

Invite the boy and his family to meet with you any time they need to talk. They'll find encouragement in your warm, friendly, nonjudgmental acceptance. Frequent contact will reinforce this encouragement. You may serve as an advocate and mediator as you help the boy tell his parents or the girl's parents. Being an advocate doesn't mean that you approve of the behavior that caused the pregnancy. You'll simply remind the parents of how much they love their son and of their desire to be caring, supportive parents. You may need to be an advocate in your church and youth group to ensure that the boy is still warmly accepted in your family of faith.

Finally, you'll need to be assertive with a teenage dad concerning his responsibilities. Without beating him down with guilt, remind him that it takes two to get pregnant and that those two both need to be involved in the pregnancy and the life of the child who may be born. You can empower the young man to be a good father by working with him to define and accept his own role as a dad.

1. Has the pregnancy been confirmed by a doctor?

2. How far along is the pregnancy?

3. Have you told your family? Do you need some help doing this?

4. Have you seen a doctor to be tested for sexually transmitted diseases or other health problems that might affect the baby?

5. What's it like for you to know your girlfriend is pregnant?

6. Would you like to know about community support programs for teenage dads?

7. Which of these feelings seem to best identify how you feel about the pregnancy?

scared	worried	important	angry	sad
excited	stupid	loved	alone	

8. What are the pros and cons of each of these options?

	PROS	CONS
stay, marry, and be a dad		
stay, be friends, and be a dad		
leave to pursue own life		
stay but keep distant from Mom and child		

9. What can I do to help?

This Week

Read Psalm 139. What can you learn about your girlfriend's pregnancy from this psalm? In what ways does this psalm encourage you?

35. Insights: Teenage Mom

What to Look For — You may hear news of a pregnancy in your youth group from the girl herself, her parents, her friends, or her boyfriend. The girl may ask for support in breaking the news to her parents. The parents may consult you for support or information. Or, the pregnant girl may carry on with a "business as usual" attitude, leaving you wondering how to approach her.

What to Say — If the girl, the parents, or the boyfriend approaches you, say: "This must be quite a shock for you. What can I do to help?"

If you're approaching a pregnant girl, say, "I understand that you're pregnant, and I was wondering if there is anything I can do to help."

What to Expect — In either scenario, expect a quick acceptance of your invitation. While some teenagers tend to glamorize pregnancy for the attention it brings, this is a cataclysmic time in the lives of the people involved. Unmarried teenagers often do get gifts and special attention when the pregnancy becomes known and in the first few days after the birth of the baby. But for the most part, pregnancy is lonely, frightening, and difficult. The girl and her family will usually welcome your stable support and friendship.

How to Respond
- First, inquire about the health of the mom-to-be. See if she has seen a doctor. If not, encourage her to make an appointment as soon as possible. Because teenagers are at high risk of delivering low birth-weight babies, early prenatal care is essential.
- Ask the teenager what she plans to do about the pregnancy. It may be too early for her to have a clear direction, but it's a decision she can't put off. You may be instrumental in helping the girl and her family make the difficult choices that need to be made.
- Be prepared to refer the girl and her family for counseling, medical services, or support services such as a young-moms group.

How Not to Respond
- Even though you may have taught about the physical and spiritual consequences of premarital sex, this is not the time to say, "I told you so." Choose grace as your response.
- None of the choices facing a pregnant teenager is easy. Don't push the girl or her family into the choice you prefer. Speak of grace, forgiveness, and God's provision. But remember that the teenager is responsible to God for her own actions. You can't take responsibility for her. The decision is ultimately the girl's and her family's. They have to live with the consequences.
- Gather information so you know what needs to happen next. It's extremely important to refer a pregnant teenager for medical care and support services. You also need to allow time for the girl and her family to just talk about the pregnancy.

How to Follow Up — Invite the girl and her family to meet with you any time they want to talk. They'll find encouragement in your warm, friendly, nonjudgmental acceptance. Frequent contact will reinforce this encouragement. You may serve as an advocate and mediator as you help the girl break the news to her parents. Being an advocate doesn't mean that you approve of the behavior that caused the pregnancy. You'll simply remind the parents of how much they love their daughter and of their desire to be caring, supportive parents. You may also need to be an advocate in your church and youth group to ensure that the girl is still warmly accepted in your family of faith.

1. Has your pregnancy been confirmed by a doctor?

2. How far along are you in your pregnancy?

3. Have you told your family? Do you need some help doing this?

4. Have you begun regular visits to a doctor?

5. What's it like for you to be pregnant?

6. Would you like to know about community support programs for teenage moms?

7. Which of these feelings seem to best identify how you feel about your pregnancy?

   scared   worried   important   angry   sad
   excited   stupid   loved   alone

8. What are the pros and cons of each of these options?

	PROS	CONS
adoption		
abortion		
single parenthood		
married parenthood		

9. What can I do to help?

This Week

Read Psalm 139. What can you learn about your pregnancy from this psalm? In what ways does this psalm encourage you?

36. Insights: Thought Disorders

What to Look For — It's unlikely that you'll have many occasions to work with an adolescent who has problems with thought disorders. However, you'll need to know how to recognize and deal with a thought-disordered teenager should one become part of your youth group. A variety of behaviors and beliefs fit into the category of thought disorders. They include

- irrational beliefs, such as thinking that others can hear their thoughts;
- the belief that they're controlled by others or by an intangible power;
- the fear that someone, such as the FBI, is plotting against them; and
- hearing voices or seeing things that no one else can hear or see.

Parents of the student may address the issue with you. If they have not, and you are aware of the problem, we recommend that you take time to talk with them. For further information on this issue, refer to "Thought Disorders" in Part Three.

What to Say — "I understand that _____ is having difficulties. I would like to help any way that I can. Since I will be working with him (her) in our youth group, can you help me understand what he (she) is going through?"

What to Expect — You may find that the parents welcome your questions and interest in their child. But because people with thought disorders are often ridiculed, avoided, or tragically labeled as "crazy" by those who do not understand the problem, the parents may want to keep the problem under wraps.

The thought-disordered teenager might be hesitant to talk to you about the problem but may respond well to your attention and encouragement.

How to Respond — Be sensitive to the parents' request to keep their child's disorder a secret. Indicate that you would like to better understand the teenager's problems. If the student has active episodes, ask for advice about what to do if an episode happens when the student is with you. Let the student know that you want to be as supportive and helpful as you can.

If you observe irrational thoughts, don't attempt to reason or argue with the student. Let the student know that you realize he or she is experiencing something you have trouble understanding. If the student becomes anxious and confused, respond with calming words and actions. In the case of bizarre behavior, you may have to call the parents and ask them to come and help you with their child.

How Not to Respond
- Don't call attention to the student if he or she has an active episode while others are around.
- Don't respond in anger or fear. This will only make the episode worse.
- Don't blame the student for disrupting your meeting. Realize that these kids have little control of their symptoms.
- When these kids are doing well, don't give them special treatment. This will only intensify their feelings of loneliness.

How to Follow Up — When you're working with a thought-disordered teenager, your main role is to provide encouragement. It's important for you to give parents feedback about their child's progress. Make it a point to share positive things as well as behaviors that concern you. Become well-informed about thought disorders. As you gain a better understanding of the issues, you'll be able to provide the family with valuable support.

(for parents)

1. Can you help me understand the problems your child is experiencing?

2. Do I need to be aware of any medication he (she) may be on? Are there side effects that I need to watch for?

3. I know that this must be difficult for you. How are you coping with it?

4. What can I do to help you and your child?

This Week

Read Romans 15:4-7. When has God given you patience and endurance beyond your human capabilities? How does Christ's acceptance of us help you be accepting of your child and his (her) problems?

(for teenagers)

1. I know you're frustrated at times when dealing with voices or confusing thoughts. How are you doing now?

2. Can you help me understand how you feel and how you deal with the things you experience?

3. How can I help you now? How can I help when things get confusing or frustrating for you?

This Week

Read Romans 15:4-5. When is it important for others to be patient with you? How can the endurance God gives you help you deal with this problem?

Copyright © Tom Klaus and Lamar Roth. Published in *Counseling Helpsheets* by Group Publishing, Inc., Box 481, Loveland, CO 80539.

Part Three:
MAKING REFERRALS AND REPORTS

Making Referrals: When and How

Some problems and issues of adolescence are outside the boundaries of pastoral care. Knowing the limits of your abilities is as important as knowing your strengths. It's to your advantage and in the best interest of the kids in your care to learn when and how to refer a student to a mental-health professional.

People in ministry often assume that they're called to be all things to all people. While we can certainly show care and concern for all the kids in our ministry, it's impossible to equip ourselves to deal with every problem that might come up in their lives.

In 1 Corinthians 12:4, Paul speaks of different gifts given to different people. Let this concept free you to refer a teenager in your ministry to a professional therapist for appropriate treatment when you lack the training or qualifications to deal with the problem yourself.

You may run across people who come to you for help but are unwilling to admit the seriousness of their problems. They may express anger or disappointment when you make a report or attempt to make a referral. Don't let these relationship issues stand in the way of making a decision in the student's best interest. Any problems resulting from referrals or reports can be dealt with after the adolescent is safe and in the appropriate treatment program or facility.

THE REFERRAL PROCESS

Making a referral can be a difficult decision for pastors and youth workers. If you're struggling with whether or not to refer an individual, consider contacting a colleague for his or her opinion. But remember that confidentiality is essential and avoid identifying the student in question.

Take time to discover the resources available to you. Get acquainted with the community mental-health center that serves your area. You may find that this agency offers a variety of services and takes all forms of payment. Many such agencies charge fees on a sliding scale according to income.

Also, make it a point to find qualified people in your area who provide counseling and psychotherapy services through private practice. People in your church and colleagues in ministry may have this information.

Serious disorders and dangerous behavior may require that the affected person be hospitalized. It's wise to become informed about psychiatric hospitals and hospitals with psychiatric units that provide services for adolescents. In most cases, you won't provide a direct referral, but you may make helpful suggestions to families who are in need of such services.

Many communities have resource directories listing the mental-health service agencies and individuals in private practice in your area. To locate these directories, contact your county health department, hospital auxiliary, chamber of commerce, community mental-health center, or department of social services. If no such directory exists, consider compiling one for your own reference or asking one of the previously mentioned agencies to develop one. You'll find the information you need in the telephone book or through hospitals, doctors, ministry colleagues, or workshops and presentations in your area.

Even when an adolescent's problem is beyond your ability and training, you'll find that your caring support and advice are still extremely important. Encourage the adolescent to talk about the problem with his or her parents. Problems tend to be resolved most quickly when parents and kids work together instead of harboring their individual secrets. Most professionals need parental consent before they can provide therapeutic services.

Families may want to find their own therapists and support groups. Or, you may advise them of available resources. But remember, it is not your responsibility to get them into treatment. Many people are skeptical and fearful of getting involved in therapy. Your patience and support will be helpful as families struggle with making decisions and choosing sources of treatment.

If you find yourself in a situation in which you believe someone is in imminent danger, it's appropriate to take an active role by making a report to authorities in order to assure the person's safety.

MAKING REPORTS

In cases of abuse, neglect, or threat of physical harm, it's your legal responsibility to make a report to the proper authorities. Most people in ministry suffer a fair amount of anxiety about taking this step. You may second-guess yourself and invest a considerable amount of emotional energy in the process. It's helpful to know that in most cases the identity of the person who makes the report is kept confidential. However, we usually inform parents and adolescents of our intention to make a report. Of course, if you feel that making your intention known would place the adolescent in danger, keep your decision to yourself.

You are bound ethically and, in many cases, legally to make reports. Don't fall into the trap of perpetuating the secret of abuse or neglect by promising to keep the information to yourself. The types of abuse you may encounter are physical, sexual, emotional, and psychological. The reporting laws vary from state to state. However, in most areas you are required to report suspicions of abuse to your local department of human services or law-enforcement agency. *Suspicions* is the key word. It's not your job to investigate or to verify that abuse has occurred. If you have any information that would lead you to suspect abuse has occurred, then you *must* make the report. The same is true when you believe a child is being willfully neglected by a parent or guardian.

If you feel that someone's life is in danger, act immediately. In the case of a suicidal teenager, you may not have much time to ponder the situation.

1. Abuse—Physical and/or Sexual

Nate is a 12-year-old who has been attending your youth group for about four months. He seems to demand a lot of attention from his peers. You've noticed that he gets angry very quickly and on one occasion threatened to beat up another boy when a game of volleyball became a little too physical. At a recent swimming party, you saw an oval bruise about 4 inches in diameter on his back. When you asked about it, he shrugged and said he was hit at school during PE. Later a group of his friends came to you, saying that Nate said his father hits him when he doesn't do as he is told. Is Nate a victim of physical abuse? Is he afraid or embarrassed to tell you about it?

Headlines and news reports provide somber daily reminders that humans can be cruel and vicious toward one another. The innocent and helpless are victimized the most. The kids in your church fall into that innocent and helpless category.

Unexplained bruises or welts on a child's body are indicators of possible physical abuse. Sometimes the shape of the mark may indicate the article used to inflict the injury. Unexplained burns, fractures, lacerations, or abrasions may also indicate that a child is being abused.

In addition to physical indicators, you may run across behavioral indicators of abuse. Kids who are being physically abused may be wary of adults. They may display behavioral extremes such as excessive withdrawal or aggressiveness. They may arrive early for youth group and stay late in an effort to avoid going home. Such behavior may also indicate sexual abuse.

In 2 Samuel 13:1-22 we find a biblical account of rape and sexual abuse that parallels the experiences of many modern children and adolescents. Amnon, King David's son, lusted after his half-sister Tamar. Amnon developed a scheme to entice Tamar to his bedroom and force her to have sex with him. Tamar suffered tremendous social and emotional trauma. Many kids today are similarly enticed, manipulated, embarrassed, and threatened. Because of fear, shame, and family loyalty, they may choose not to disclose what's happening to them.

In our experience both as ministers and as professional therapists, we've encountered many children and adolescents who have been sexually abused. Our response is always the same: We feel sickened, angry, and empathetic, and we wish the situation would go away. But we know that it won't and that we must confront the issues head on.

Your role in cases of sexual abuse is to make a report, not to provide counseling or conduct an investigation. You'll find it difficult to determine if someone in your ministry is being sexually abused unless the individual, family, or friends tell you. Behavioral indicators include an unwillingness to participate in group activities, the presence of sexually transmitted diseases, withdrawal, unusual fantasies, bizarre sexual behavior or knowledge, poor peer relationships, and depression.

The time may come when a student feels the need to disclose to someone the fact that he or she is being abused. The student may tell a friend, who in turn shares the information with you. Or, the student may tell you directly. For the safety of the student, you need to report the information to the authorities immediately.

In a case like Nate's, you might share with him what his friends told you. Then ask him if his father is hitting him. You have an obligation to report to authorities your *suspicion* that Nate is being physically abused at home. It's difficult to ask a student if he or she has been or is being physically or sexually abused. However, the potential benefits to the adolescent far outweigh the risks.

You aren't required to investigate possible abuse. Avoid the urge to "get to the bottom" of a situation like Nate's for two reasons. First, the investigation needs to be handled by someone who is trained to gather information without contamination such as asking leading questions, offering suggestions, or making assumptions. The second reason is that Nate and his family need you to minister to them. Assuming the role of an investigator could compromise your ability to encourage and support the family during this difficult time.

During the disclosure, the goals are for the abuse to stop, for the individuals involved to experience emotional and spiritual healing, and for the family to experience healing. Several key players may have a role in reaching these goals: law-enforcement officers, social-service agents, therapists, and ministers. Your role will be to continue to provide support and spiritual guidance. Many times the victim and family members feel a need to share their pain in a nonthreatening environment. This may happen in therapy with a professional counselor or with you in the context of your ministry.

As you listen with your ears, eyes, and heart, you'll reinforce the supportive nature of the church and help family members feel that they're not alone. It's extremely important to keep your conversations confiden-

tial. You may hear things that you feel the therapist should know. Encourage the family or individual to share the information with the therapist as well.

In some cases, the person who is abusing the adolescent may be removed temporarily from the home. This absence can cause a host of emotional, functional, and financial problems. A caring pastor and congregation can step in and provide emotional support, financial gifts, help with transportation, and child care. With a watchful eye you may discover other areas in which your ministry may be effective and appreciated.

2. Attention Deficit (Hyperactivity) Disorder, AD(H)D

Y*ou don't have to look up to know that Tim has arrived at youth group. He thumps three people on the back, then goes over to the Ping-Pong table and starts commenting loudly on a game that's already in progress. When you call the group together to begin Bible study, Tim is the last one to take a seat. He doesn't even pretend to open his Bible. Instead, he doodles on the soles of his tennis shoes with a ballpoint pen. Then he starts drumming on the metal chair in front of him and draws an angry look from the girl sitting in that chair. The only contribution Tim makes to the discussion is to mock someone or throw in a sarcastic remark. You have a much easier time handling the group when Tim isn't around, and you wonder why he even bothers to come.*

If Tim has attention deficit (hyperactivity) disorder, it may be very difficult for him to control the behaviors that annoy you and the kids in your youth group. AD(H)D has received a lot of attention in the last few years. Many professionals complain that it's over-diagnosed, while just as many believe it's under-diagnosed. We've found the identification of AD(H)D to be useful and the treatment fairly successful.

A student with AD(H)D will often exhibit varying degrees of inattention, impulsiveness, and hyperactive behavior. Many children begin exhibiting these behaviors around age 4. Parents often report that their child has been overactive since he or she was a toddler. You may also run across students who have attention deficit disorder but are not hyperactive. These kids may "fall through the cracks," because even though they have difficulty focusing on tasks, their quiet behavior doesn't command a teacher's or group leader's attention.

Kids with AD(H)D have a difficult time focusing on a task in the presence of even the slightest distraction. They may move from one task to the next without satisfactorily completing anything. They often have difficulty following rules of a game and will tend to cut in line and constantly interrupt others. AD(H)D children may appear fidgety and unable to sit still for boring tasks. They may be unable to follow instructions and may rush through a task just to get it over with.

Researchers believe that AD(H)D has a strong biological component. It's possible that in some cases the disorder is inherited. The treatment for AD(H)D frequently consists of a combined effort by parents, physicians, school personnel, and therapists. The child may be taking one of several medications. The most common are the psycho-stimulants Ritalin, Cylert, and Dexedrine. Recently, doctors have begun to prescribe anti-depressants such as Tofranil and Norpramine, as well as the anti-hypertensive Catapres and the anti-convulsant Tegretol. It's good to be aware of the medications AD(H)D kids in your youth group are taking.

Most parents appreciate feedback from adults who provide supervision and care for their AD(H)D children. The professionals providing treatment constantly monitor the child's progress and the effects of the medication. Your insights may be helpful to them.

Instead of labeling these adolescents as troublemakers, accept them as individuals who are struggling with a problem that's primarily biological. In addition to medication, behavior modification also appears to be useful. It's appropriate to ask parents about what kind of helping role you can play with their AD(H)D child.

One effective way to deal with AD(H)D kids is to gently redirect their attention. Try to minimize distractions as much as possible. Keep in mind that these kids tend to respond well to praise and goal setting. Sometimes it's best to ignore some aggressive or hyperactive behaviors that bother you. If you notice that the adolescent is unable to remain focused during group meetings, speak with the parents and find out if the child is taking medication only during school hours. If so, the doctor may be willing to adjust the dosage to cover youth group as well.

Some children take the medication only during the school year. This may also need to be re-evaluated. If you plan a weekend outing or camp, speak with the parents about the medication schedule. Usually kids manage their own medication. However, there may be times when parents ask you to be responsible for administering the proper dosage.

Overall, AD(H)D kids can be a challenge. You can be helpful by understanding what AD(H)D is and cooperating with the treatment. Keep in touch with the parents, both to gain insights on dealing with the child and to provide feedback.

3. Conduct Disorders

*T*he phone rings at 1:00 a.m. The father of a teenager in your youth group says: "We just received a call from the police, and Jason has been picked up again. He broke into a store and took some things. Then he led the police on a chase. No one is hurt, but could you come with us to pick him up? We're at our wits' end and don't know what to do."

We've experienced many such calls as ministers and therapists. Perhaps you have, too.

The adolescent whose life appears to be careening out of control is frustrating and difficult to deal with. Conduct disorders consist of a wide range of behaviors such as stealing, forgery, running away, lying, fire setting, skipping school, breaking and entering, destroying property, cruelty to animals, rape or sexual molestation, fighting with or without weapons, robbery, and other types of physical cruelty to others.[4]

These behaviors frustrate and baffle those trying to help the adolescent. When you see these patterns developing, it's time to refer this family for professional help.

Many factors can contribute to the development of conduct disorders. The family may be experiencing ongoing conflict, not the least of which is the teenager's problem behavior. There may also be marital conflicts, inappropriate parenting, health problems, and financial problems, just to name a few.

Other forces may also be at work in the adolescent's life. Influences in the community, success or failure at school, and peer pressure also seem to be key factors that may draw teenagers into severe conduct disorders. Early professional intervention, usually in the form of family and group therapy, is important. In extreme cases, it's necessary to remove the child from the home and place him or her in a foster home, a juvenile-correction facility, or a group home. Early intervention may prevent the need for such drastic measures.

Sometimes working with an adolescent who's exhibiting conduct disorders may leave you feeling powerless. You may be rejected, criticized, and ignored. You may also hear all the right words but see no change in behavior. Unless the adolescent and family are ready to accept your help, there's little you can do. In fact, the situation and behaviors may become worse before they become better.

The key for a youth worker trying to minister to these kids is: *Don't give up!* That's what most of the other adults in these kids' lives have done, so that's what they'll expect from you. But hang in there. These kids have a deep need to be accepted regardless of their faults and behavior. Unconditional love is the best medicine.

Listening is important. It's a difficult task when the student isn't willing to share much and you feel you're not being appreciated. Take time to listen to what the student *doesn't* say, as well as to what he or she does say. Be slow to criticize; this person has already been criticized to the extreme. Obviously, you don't want to approve the destructive, negative behavior, but you can help the teenager put things into perspective. You can also talk about some of the forces we've already mentioned that may draw the student in to negative behavior. But keep in mind that the choices an adolescent makes are his own or her own responsibility.

Decision making is difficult when

emotions are high and the teenager feels pulled in several directions at once. Yet, one of the most important qualities these kids need to develop is the ability to take responsibility for their behavior. We don't want to make the mistake of allowing teenagers to dodge responsibility for their behavior by stating that they're merely products of their environment. This is a gross injustice to the person who desperately needs to develop control over his or her behavior. Instead, we need to help them through decision-making processes when they're ready and willing to cooperate. This approach develops teenagers' personal integrity—a quality that's often lacking.

Low self-worth begins to change when a student feels accepted and loved. Significant people in the student's life need to note and affirm positive behaviors as they develop. You are one of those significant people. Your support is very important.

Never rescue the teenager from the consequences of his or her behavior. Suffering negative consequences can be a great motivator for the teenager to find help in order to avoid further consequences.

You can play a significant, positive role in the lives of kids with severe conduct problems. Remember, there's no substitute for patience and persistence. The results come slowly, but when they do happen, the rewards are tremendous.

4. Depression

arl's parents ask if you can meet with them on Saturday morning. As they enter your office, you notice their somber, concerned expressions. Carl's mother begins by telling you that Carl has changed. He's no longer the happy-go-lucky person he was several months earlier. He withdraws from the family and spends a lot of time in his room. He eats very little and seems to sleep whenever he has the chance. The parents ask you to talk with Carl tomorrow afternoon to find out what's getting him down.

The next day, you meet Carl at his home. Initially Carl reports that things are OK. However, when you share his parents' concerns, Carl begins to cry silently. He says that he doesn't know why he's feeling so sad. He finds himself crying a lot and is embarrassed to be around others when he feels this way. He thinks if he could only get a grip on himself, he'd feel better.

Depression is a difficult problem to assess because of the wide range of feelings and behaviors it can encompass. There are several types of depression. In general, a major depressive episode consists of a depressed mood or irritability, a lack of interest in activities that were once pleasurable, a change in eating habits, excessive sleeping, insomnia, energy loss, feelings of worthlessness, an inability to concentrate, and thoughts of death or suicide.[5]

The first step in dealing with depression is for the student to have a complete physical examination in order to rule out a physical problem. Most depressed kids won't be able to "pull themselves up by their bootstraps." Depressed kids need help.

Depression may be a reaction to a traumatic event such as the loss of a loved one. Bipolar or manic depression may come and go with dramatic mood swings. A full-blown, major depressive episode can last for months. In a case such as Carl's, you would be wise to suggest that Carl's parents schedule a complete physical, then meet with a professional therapist or counselor.

When you become aware that an adolescent in your group has been diagnosed as clinically depressed, your role will be to support and nurture both the student and parents. The student will appreciate your encouragement during the emotional ups and downs he or she experiences. Medication may leave the student feeling drowsy or dry-mouthed. Encourage the student to stay involved in positive peer relationships. Don't accept negative self-statements from the student. Instead, affirm his or her positive attributes. Let the student know that you genuinely care and are interested in his or her progress.

Working with a depressed adolescent can take a lot of energy. But the rewards are well-worth the effort for you, for the adolescent, and for his or her family.

*L*indsay is a 16-year-old girl from a middle-class family. She's a popular person in your youth group—a high school sophomore who appears to be successful in academics. Lately you've noticed that she's become moody and appears to be sickly. Her friend Sarah comes to you after church one evening and tells you that she's observed Lindsay throwing up after meals on several occasions over the past few weeks. She says that Lindsay just laughs and says that some things make her sick. Sarah is worried, and so are you.

Lindsay may be suffering from an eating disorder called anorexia nervosa. The symptoms include a refusal to maintain normal body weight or a failure to make expected weight gains during growth periods, a fear of becoming fat, being underweight yet feeling fat, or the absence of three consecutive menstrual periods. Anorexic kids may overexercise, use laxatives, purge after meals, refuse to eat, or employ all or a combination of these approaches.[6]

Bulimia nervosa is another eating disorder characterized by binge eating (consuming large amounts of food in a short time), self-induced vomiting, and feelings of a lack of self-control related to eating. Kids with this problem may also use laxatives, fast, or overexercise. The binge eating is usually done in private and kept a secret.[7]

Anorexia and bulimia behaviors are similar. Some adolescents may exhibit both sets of symptoms. Don't attempt to make a diagnosis. Instead, express your concerns about these behaviors to the individual and her parents. Suggest a complete physical examination. If the examining physician makes a diagnosis of anorexia or bulimia, it's time to make a referral to a professional who specializes in the treatment of these disorders.

You can play an important role in the life of a teenager in your youth group who's been diagnosed with an eating disorder. Reinforce the self-worth of the teenager. Encourage communication between parents and child. Take special care to involve the adolescent in youth programs, since she may tend to withdraw from social situations. The parents and teenager will welcome your consistent encouragement and support.

6. Substance Abuse

*S*andy used to attend youth group regularly, but since her mother deserted the family two years ago, she's nearly dropped out of sight. You've heard from other kids that Sandy hates her stepmother and says her house is like a war zone. At the mall, you notice Sandy hanging around with a rough-looking bunch of kids. You barely recognize her—her face is hard, and she seems much older. Next, you hear that Sandy's been expelled from school for missing classes. A month later, Sandy's father comes to your office with the news that Sandy and her friends were arrested in a drug bust. He wants you to go with him to post bond for her.

There's nothing more tragic than watching a teenager self-destruct by abusing or becoming dependent on drugs or alcohol. Our focus here will not be on kids who experiment with these substances, even though such experimentation is certainly dangerous. Instead, we'll deal with adolescents who regularly abuse these substances or have become dependent on them.

You may be alerted to abuse or dependence problems in a variety of ways. Kids in your group may relate stories about so-and-so's drinking or drug usage. Parents may come to you with concerns about their child's behavior. Kids may get into trouble with the law. Or, you may notice that an adolescent's life is crumbling and suspect that substance abuse or dependence is at the root of the problem.

When you see a teenager in your group struggling with substance abuse, the first step is to make a referral to a professional therapist who deals with these issues. This is a difficult step for many parents and teenagers because it forces them to admit that there's a problem. In most cases, the therapist will make an evaluation and determine the extent of the problem and the most effective treatment.

As a minister or youth worker, your support and spiritual guidance at this point are extremely important. Check in with the family and the teenager occasionally to find out about the teenager's progress or lack of progress. This contact allows the people involved to accept the problem and to be accepted by others who know the problem exists. Encourage participation in support groups such as Alcoholics Anonymous and Narcotics Anonymous in which the student will have the opportunity to accept the problem and take responsibility for his or her drinking or drug usage.

Substance abuse often results in conduct disorders. For further guidance on how to support teenagers and families who are experiencing the pain of substance abuse, review the discussion of conduct disorders beginning on page 106 of Part Three.

Sam: Lately I've been wondering if it's all worth it.
You: What is it that may not be worth it?
Sam: Life—you know what I mean?
You: Are you thinking of hurting yourself?
Sam: Well . . .

This could be one of the most frightening conversations you ever have. Even when you leave the conversation with reasonable assurance that the adolescent will not commit suicide, you may still experience a nagging fear. "Did I do enough? Did he say he would not kill himself just to get me off of his back? Could I and should I have done something more?"

When students come to us for help, we always ask: "Are you having suicidal thoughts? Have you ever seriously contemplated suicide?" If kids respond positively to the second question, we'll monitor their thoughts as we progress in treatment. If kids are *currently* experiencing suicidal thoughts, we carefully assess the level of risk.

When you work with suicidal adolescents, you take on a tremendous responsibility. It's important to make a referral to a professional therapist immediately. If the individual indicates that he or she is going to act on the suicidal thoughts, contact a local law-enforcement agency at once. Share as much information as possible: the teenager's name, address, telephone number, age, plan of suicide, and present location. Time is of the essence. In such cases, confidentiality is waived in the effort to save the student's life.

Always be alert to indicators of potentially suicidal behavior. Some kids may make slightly veiled verbal threats of suicide. Always take them seriously. You may hear an ambiguous threat such as "You won't have to worry about me much longer." Pay attention to these threats. Clarify the student's intent by confronting him or her directly. Ask, "What do you mean by that?" Let students know that you genuinely want to help by getting them to a qualified counselor or therapist. You may be tipped off to suicidal intent by behavioral indicators such as a dramatic change in mood, difficulty concentrating, sudden alcohol or drug usage, sudden problems at school or at home, and personality changes.

As a youth worker, be aware of major changes or disruptions in the lives of the kids in your group. These might include a breakup with a boyfriend or girlfriend, the loss of a significant loved one through death or distance, or marital conflict between parents. This quick checklist may help you to identify a teenager at risk of suicide.

- Is the student depressed?
- Has the student attempted suicide in the past?
- Has a significant person in the student's life, such as a parent or sibling, attempted or committed suicide?
- Is depression common in the student's family?

If you can answer yes to one or more of these questions, the student may be at risk and will possibly struggle with suicidal thoughts at some point during adolescence.

Any time you become aware of a teenager with a suicide plan, you *must* contact the local law-enforcement agency. That agency will place the teenager in a protective environment. When the imminent danger has passed, appropriate therapy can be initiated. Your emotional and spiritual support can play a significant role in helping the student and family get through this difficult time in their lives.

8. Thought Disorders

Terry is a 15-year-old boy who's a member of your youth group. His parents attend your church and appear to have a normal family life. However, Terry has always been a bit different. Lately, he's been withdrawn and depressed. He seems frustrated and preoccupied with themes of death and violence. One Sunday, Terry's parents share with you that he is in therapy and may have to go to a psychiatric hospital for an evaluation because he's been troubled by thoughts he can't control.

Thought disorders may be the result of several problems. People with thought disorders may experience auditory hallucinations—hearing voices that tell them to do things or that comment on their behavior or characteristics. Their emotions may seem flat, even when a situation would normally evoke some kind of emotional response.

The most difficult thought disorder to treat is schizophrenia. People with this disorder may have delusions and irrational beliefs such as believing others can hear their thoughts, that others are controlling them, that their thoughts are not their own, or that others are plotting against them.

Schizophrenia can eventually become debilitating in several areas of the adolescent's life. The treatment most often includes a combination of anti-psychotic medication to help control the disturbing thought processes, and family therapy to help address adjustments to and acceptance of the disorder. No cure for schizophrenia exists at this time. Most people with this diagnosis must accept the probability that they will have to deal with it throughout their lives.

Your role is to help provide these kids with normal life experiences as much as possible. There may be periods when you don't notice any problems at all. Other times you may witness depression and active hallucinations. If you begin to notice such behavior, notify the parents, who can then relay the information to doctors or therapists involved in the treatment.

Thought disorders may coincide with depression. People suffering from thought disorders may experience hallucinations or delusions which tend to be related to the depression. For example, a depressed student may hear a voice that tells him to kill himself, or a depressed girl might hear a voice telling her that she is not a worthwhile person. Sometimes the voices may say things not related to the depression; however, this is not the usual pattern. As the depression is alleviated, the thoughts usually decrease or disappear.

The seriousness of thought disorders certainly calls for professional treatment. However, you can provide important support and encouragement to the thought-disordered adolescent and his or her family. Give the family feedback when you notice progress or setbacks in the child's symptoms. If you notice symptoms of thought disorders in a teenager who has not been diagnosed, discuss the symptoms with the adolescent and parents. You may be able to provide a helpful referral to an appropriate professional who can initiate testing in order to make a clear diagnosis.

ENDNOTES

1. *Diagnostic and Statistical Manual of Mental Disorders,* revised third edition (Washington, D.C.: American Psychiatric Association, 1987), 55.
2. Ibid., 222.
3. Ibid., 67-69.
4. Ibid., 55.
5. Ibid., 222.
6. Ibid., 67.
7. Ibid., 68-69.